Breaking Barriers: Women in Leadership

Henry J. Furlong

Abstract

In the phenomenological qualitative study, "The Female Leadership Gap: Breaking Down the Barriers and Biases of Women in Leadership," the phenomenological qualitative study explored leadership from the perspectives and lived experiences of women leaders in governmental organizations and private industries. This dissertation was an examination to increase comprehension of factors that impact executive-level women while striving to achieve senior positions. Utilizing semi-structured interviews, data were collected through electronic correspondences, virtual platform interviews, and field notes. Data were analyzed through multiple levels of coding. This phenomenological qualitative study utilized a purposeful sample of 13 participants. Within the chapters of this dissertation, the purpose, problem, and methodology are examined to determine what methods may alleviate the barriers and biases contributing to the underrepresentation of women in leadership positions. This dissertation provided a unique opportunity for women from various levels of leadership and occupations to share their ideas, feelings, and perceptions of aspects of professional life collectively experienced by women. This research contributed to the conversation on the paucity of women in senior leadership positions and the outcomes of women's leadership development. The gender leadership gap is significant, and women's representation in leadership will not increase substantially without major changes in the organizations' culture and policies.

Keywords: barriers, biases, gender, leadership, phenomenology, role congruity theory, underrepresentation

Table of Contents

Tables 8

Figures 9

CHAPTER 1: INTRODUCTION 10

    Background of Problem 12

    Statement of the Problem 15

    Rationale 16

    Contribution of the Study 17

    Research Questions 18

    Process to Accomplish 19

    Conceptual Framework for a Qualitative Study 22

    Definition of Terms 24

    Limitations and Delimitations 26

    Chapter Summary 29

CHAPTER 2: LITERATURE REVIEW 30

    Barriers to Advancement 32

    Organizational Culture 35

    Discrimination in Economic Systems 37

    Occupational Segregation 44

    Role Congruity Theory 45

    Leadership Theory 49

Gender Stereotypes in the Workplace 51

Rate of Change of Women in Leadership Positions 53

Biblical Integration 64

Chapter Summary 64

CHAPTER 3: RESEARCH METHODOLOGY 67

Research Method and Design 69

Participants 72

Instrument(s) 74

Research Procedures 80

Data Analysis Strategy 81

Delimitations 83

Ethical Issues 83

Chapter Summary 84

CHAPTER 4: ANALYSIS & RESULTS 85

Descriptive Data 87

Education Status of Participants 91

Pursuing Higher Education 93

Participation in Mentorship Programs 93

Data Analysis Procedures 95

Data Collection 95

Data Transcription 97

Research Questions 99

Results 107

Summary of Core Themes 108

Gender Preferences 109

Politics 110

Religion 112

Education 114

Ethnicity 117

Chapter Summary 118

CHAPTER 5: CONCLUSIONS AND SUGGESTIONS FOR FURTHER STUDY 120

Summary of Study 122

Overview 123

Conclusions & Discussions 126

Theoretical Implications 127

Practical and Future Implications 128

Strengths & Weaknesses 132

Recommendations for Future Research 136

Chapter Summary 140

Tables

Table 1: Research Questions and Interview Question Chart 76

Table 2: Qualitative Plan 77

Table 3: Demographic Data 89

Table 4: Age of the Participants 90

Table 5: Analysis Procedure of Data Collected 97

Table 6: Research Question 1 Quotations 100

Table 7: Research Question 2 Quotations 101

Table 8: Research Question 3 Quotations 102

Table 9: Research Question 4 Quotations 105

Table 10: Research Question 5 Quotations 107

Table 11: Dominant Themes: Gender Preference 110

Table 12: Dominant Themes: Politics 112

Table 13: Dominant Themes: Religion 114

Table 14: Dominant Themes: Education 116

Table 15: Dominant Themes: Ethnicity 118

Table 16: Emerging Themes 135

Figures

Figure 1: Age of Participants 91

Figure 2: Education Level of Participants 92

Figure 3: Participants Pursuing Higher Education 92

Figure 4: Participation in Mentorship Programs 93

Figure 5: Sector of Operation 94

Figure 6: Affiliation with Female Leadership Organizations 94

CHAPTER 1: INTRODUCTION

The Female Leadership Gap: Breaking Down the Biases and Barriers of Women in Leadership

The current literature regarding feminism includes several approaches to understanding the differences between men and women and addressing equality and opportunity (Painter-Morland & Desleandes, 2014). In the leadership realm, the equality discourse has often confronted women with the challenge to simply do what men have always been able to do to ensure the task at hand was completed and successfully (Painter-Morland & Desleandes, 2014). According to Painter-Morland and Desleandes (2014), men have adopted patriarchal organizations' leadership practices. As a result, female pioneers have unwittingly perpetuated male leadership stereotypes (Painter-Morland & Desleandes, 2014).

Over 40 studies conducted since the 1970s (when the United Nations launched its Decade for Women) have enabled women to emerge from the shadows (Goulart et al., 2021). There has been renaissance in the conversation surrounding women's voices in the socio-economic and political landscape. The impact of women within communities has always been prevalent and consequential (Leal Filho et al., 2021). In the political realm, women's voices are coming to the forefront of important conversations regarding women's rights and perspectives. Discussions and debates about feminism have surfaced in recent years illustrating the increasing need of women being engaged in leadership positions in all levels business and government (Ely & Padavic, 2020). Many values within the movement have been accepted across the political spectrum in the United States (Leal Filho et al., 2021). Barroso (2020) surveyed gender equality that came a century after the ratification of the 19th Amendment. Gender equality is found even among Americans who do not personally identify as feminists (Leal Filho et al., 2021).

According to Sengupta (2018), "The world is visibly split into two halves—one who perceives feminism as feminism and one who is confused between equalism vs. feminism" (para. 1). Feminist theorist seek to promote women's legal status as equal and undifferentiated from men's (Longman et al., 2018). While women have succeeded in arguing for equal rights and opportunities, efforts to bring equality to women have not fully allowed all women to develop their leadership capabilities and opportunities (Longman et al., 2018). Longman et al. (2018) stated that one of the central assumptions in many organizational practices is that women are society's caretakers. Caretaking primarily involves unpaid labor within the private sphere. In the workplace, jobs that require taking care of individuals' bodily, emotional, or domestic needs have been typically conducted by females, with an associated low level of compensation (Longman et al., 2018). Women are frequently excluded from various organizations' leadership prospects that traditionally and characteristically reach outside the caretaking realm (Painter-Morland, 2020).

According to the Bachelet (2020), a gender stereotype is a generalized view or preconception about women's and men's attributes or characteristics common in organizations. Addressing these prejudices is not an easy task (Hall, 2018). A gender stereotype is harmful when it limits women's and men's capacity to develop abilities, pursue professional careers, and make life choices (Bachelet, 2020).

The purpose of this study was to discover the female leadership gap by breaking down the biases and barriers of women in leadership specifically in governmental organizations and private industries. Within the sections of this chapter, the purpose, problem, and methodology are examined to determine how efforts can be made to alleviate the barriers and biases contributing to the underrepresentation of women in leadership positions.

Background of the Problem

Researchers have reported that, in practice, women's and men's leadership characteristics are virtually indistinguishable (Kim et al., 2018). Adler (1997) stated that the number of women leaders in business organizations had more than doubled since the 1970s, but noted that women remained underrepresented in managerial positions worldwide. According to Warner et al. (2018), in the first quarter of 2018, 27 women headed large firms in the United States, representing 5% of chief executive officers (CEOs) of Fortune 500 companies, which is a decrease from 6% in 2017. Hinchliffe indicated in his 2020 study that General Motors was the largest company in the United States to hold a female CEO. This indicates progress, as in 1995, no female CEOs were on the Fortune 500 list (Warner et al., 2018).

Chin et al. (2020) conducted a study on women's leadership at McKinsey Consulting from 2012 to 2015 and noted that women held 42% of entry-level jobs, 28% of senior-level roles, and 16% of chief executive, chief financial officer, chief operating officer, or chief information officer positions in the United States. The data showed there was no significant change between 2012 and 2015 (Chin et al., 2020). Chin et al. also found that women in senior positions were 20% less likely to leave held positions than men who held comparable jobs because of the possibility of not finding a similar position. Women are still much less likely to be hired for jobs than men, even when women have the same qualifications (Horowitz et al., 2018a). According to Horowitz et al., (2018a) research indicates that Americans perceive men and women as equally capable regarding some of the key qualities and behaviors essential for leadership. However, according to the International Labour Organization (2018), women tend to be overrepresented in occupations perceived as unskilled and low value, particularly in the healthcare industry. Lennon et al. (2013) indicated that throughout the decades, the results of female leadership research have continued to illustrate the equivalent outcomes.

As Lennon et al. (2013) noted, there appears to be a distinctive predisposition against women holding leadership positions, particularly in senior positions of organizations (Lennon et al., 2013). Selzer et al. (2017) reviewed a 2015 Pew Research study and found that 40% of those polled believed there was a double standard for women seeking executive positions. Studies have shown that systemic leadership models allow various leadership roles and styles to coexist in an organization (Painter-Morland & Desleandes, 2014). Accepting multiple roles and ensuring they do not go unnoticed and uncompensated is challenging (Painter-Morland & Desleandes, 2014).

According to Colella and King (2018), gender discrimination is rampant in the workplace, with women earning approximately "78 cents to every dollar" compared to men (p. 81). In many industries, women are less likely than men to advance to the top of fields (Colella & King, 2018). Furthermore, women comprise only 4.2% of CEOs and 19.2% of board members at S&P 500 firms (Moreno et al., 2020)

Additionally, "57% of Americans think men and women in top positions in business and politics are different when it comes to leadership styles, while 43% say women are the same" (Horowitz et al., 2018b, para. 4). However, for many years, some women have not been given top positions because of gender (Horowitz et al., 2018a, 2018b.). According to Meyerson and Fletcher (2000), the root cause of the inequity is that men have written many workplace policies, norms, and practices that cater to the male experience.

Meyerson and Fletcher (2000) also noted that women's interests and needs continue to be underrepresented or ignored altogether due to this flawed perspective. Specific "ways of doing business" are deeply entrenched and, in many respects, have become a part of organization's

DNA (Meyerson & Fletcher, 2000, p. 23). Corporate leaders define and evaluate leadership capabilities and competencies based mainly on male-dominated traits (Meyerson & Fletcher, 2000). Prejudices regarding men's and women's positions remain in society, with women now being held predominantly responsible for domestic matters rather than employment (Meyerson & Fletcher, 2000). The situation is noteworthy because "organizational practices mirror societal norms" (Meyerson & Fletcher, 2000, p. 2). The presumption does not mean that blame should be placed exclusively on men (Hoobler et al., 2018). Still, it is essential to acknowledge the origin of a contributing factor to devise and implement a workable solution (Hoobler et al., 2018).

Another explanation for the continued underrepresentation of women in leadership is that many people like to be surrounded with others who are similar (Hoobler et al., 2018). People have a natural attraction to and affinity to people perceived to share similar physical characteristics, behavior, personality, and attitudes (Hoobler et al., 2018). Thus, men in leadership, who are more comfortable with other men professionally than with women, continue to promote men up the ladder (Smith et al., 2019). Globally, however, and most specifically in the United States, there has long been a gendered division of labor (Thomas, 2020). In an attempt to deal with the disparity between women and men in the workplace, leaders in corporations throughout the United States have initiated educational programs and policies (Taylor, 2020). Schein (1973) developed the think manager–think male theory from the perceived correlation between a man's expected behavior and leaders' predicted behavior. Schein's foundational research continues to be relevant and unveils the stereotypical associations between leadership and gender. While Schein's research on stereotypes was substantiated when conducted, more recent researchers' outcomes continue to illustrate that not only do stereotypes remain in existence, but also, they remain sanctioned (Watson et al., 2018).

Statement of the Problem

Many barriers and biases contributing to the scarcity of female senior leadership in large governmental organizations and private industries across the United States remain unknown. The problem this researcher sought to address in this study is the barriers and biases of the female leadership gap, specifically in governmental organizations and private industries. According to the American Association of University Women (AAUW, 2020), "Achieving gender parity in leadership is, first and perhaps most important, a matter of fairness" (p. 2). Leaders help decide how the dynamics of society will operate moving forward. Regardless of gender, failure to promote based on ability may negatively impact society on a global scale (AAUW, 2020). Women have, indeed, made notable advancements toward achieving gender equality in the workplace, and have constituted over 46% of the labor force (Bureau of Labor Statistics, 2015). As stated in the AAUW, "men are far more likely than women to rise to the highest paying and most prestigious leadership roles in almost any industry" (p. 19). There is a leadership diversity gap in senior level positions between women and men across the country (Warner et al., 2018). According to Warner et al. (2018), the fact that women are known to perform better than men overall does not appear to impact the ability to lead. Women have outnumbered men on college campuses since 1988 (Warner et al., 2018), have earned at least one-third of law degrees since 1980, and comprised one-third of medical school students by 1990 (Warner et al., 2018).

Women leaders add value to a corporation's bottom line and do not impair it (Dezsö & Ross, 2012). Dezsö and Ross (2012) compared 15 years of S&P 500 firms' management data with and without at least one woman in top management. The firm performance improved with just one woman being present in senior leadership (Dezsö & Ross, 2012). Women tend to have strengths in balancing risk and coping with failure, coupled with such characteristics, as creativity, intelligence, and emotional stability (Watson & Detjen, 2021). Along with higher education and professional credentials, these abilities suggest women are ideal candidates for leadership (Saleem et al., 2017). reflective of their educational achievements (Warner et al., 2018).

Women's presence in top leadership positions as law partners, medical school deans, and corporate executive officers remains between 5% and 20% in a broad range of fields (Warner et al., 2018). Overall, there is an enormous gap between the fortunes of a small number of prominent women at the top of fields and most women nationwide (Warner et al., 2018). A gulf widens between American women and counterparts in peer nations (Warner et al., 2018). Although women outperform men in the number of college degrees earned, women are not appropriately represented or positioned in power and leadership (Warner et al., 2018). The problem addressed in this study is the imbalance of gender representation within senior leadership in governmental organizations and private industries across the United States and the factors contributing to this scarcity.

Rationale

In this qualitative phenomenological study, the investigation explored and described the lived experiences of women overlooked for leadership positions in the workplace. Although women outperform men in the number of educational degrees earned, women are not held at the same level in power and leadership hierarchy (Adu, 2019). The research objective was to complete an immediate investigation of the imbalance of gender representation in leadership positions. Structured questions were used to gather ideas and insights from 13 women across the United States to identify the causes of women's underrepresentation in leadership. Tables and graphs were generated to identify analysis for the interviews and to determine the leading causes of women's underrepresentation within leadership roles.

This study explored and offered a potential explanation for women's lack of representation in the workplace and discussed the glass ceiling effect as the subconscious bias on women and leadership (Lyness & Grotto, 2018). The study is relevant to demonstrating examined the smaller number of women in leadership positions than men, potentially because of gender (Martineau & Mount, 2019). The quality of women's job performance, education, and ability to balance home and work life was measured (Lyness & Grotto, 2018). This qualitative study involved interviewing women working in corporations who do not hold hierarchy leadership positions. Applying a phenomenological design lead to detailed descriptions of women in corporate and government jobs through interviews, questionnaires, and document reviews that described things as circumstances are and how they could be different. The method and design helped determine the underlying factors regarding why women are underrepresented in leadership positions and may lead to suggestions regarding ways to develop a better system for hiring the best people for leadership positions.

Contribution of Study

This study is relevant to women overlooked for promotions to leadership positions in workplaces. Women have attained degrees equal to or higher than men within the United States and perform similar to or better than the male counterparts (Manzi, 2019). This study's results may offer companies and organizations a better understanding that the women are as qualified as men to obtain leadership positions. This study's potential contribution to women's research in leadership may lead to more women being promoted to leadership roles designed for or only offered to men. This study will add to the knowledge and literature on leadership by exposing the norms that prevent women from being promoted to leadership roles. The study may also help change what attributes are considered for men and women in these roles.

Research Questions

Over 40 years have elapsed since introducing the "think manager-think male" concept from Schein's (1973, p. 94) original article regarding the perceived characteristics of leaders and gender stereotypes (as cited in Coder & Spiller, 2013). At the time of Schein's study, women accounted for about 5% of organizational leaders. In 2009, the United States Bureau of Labor Statistics reported that female representation in leadership increased to 40%; however, women only represented 2% of Fortune 500 CEOs (Coder & Spiller, 2013). This study examined the female leadership gap by breaking down the barriers and biases of women in leadership, specifically in governmental organizations and private industries to include the employees' perceptions of gender stereotypical views within places of employment. The study further explored whether stereotypical beliefs contributed to the underrepresentation of female leaders in the United States.

The following research questions were utilized to explore women's challenges with stereotypical views of female behavior as women aspired to executive leadership roles in the private and public sectors. To discover if parallels in women's experiences with bias or prejudice exist, the answers lead to various reasons for the underrepresentation of women's leadership. As women aspire to executive leadership in the private and public sectors, this could be an essential point of discovery to ensure success.

- RQ1: How do women mentorship programs influence women in attaining top leadership positions in private and political sectors?
- RQ2: What support do women need to attain successful careers as leaders?

- RQ3: How does the representation of women in higher levels of leadership impact the views and beliefs on women's leadership roles?
- RQ4: What are the various factors motivating or limiting women in attaining top leadership positions in private and public sectors?
- RQ5: How does a woman's family dynamics affect her leadership role compared to her male counterparts?

Process to Accomplish

A phenomenological design accomplished the purpose of this research. The responses to the study's research questions were collected and analyzed to determine the core issues related to women's underrepresentation in leadership positions. Analyzing the data helped identify business needs and make predictions regarding how working environments can change for women. The assumption that women retain lower-level positions because of stereotypes as mother figures or nurturers by nature leads to labeling women as too weak to hold hierarchy positions in large corporations (Law, 2020). When women are labeled, denying women promotions becomes the norm for many employers (Smith et al., 2019). Although women can move up the ladder to become leaders in organizations, many opportunities disappear at various levels of a woman's career path (Martin, 2019). According to Martin (2019), gender should not be a factor in the extent to which a person can be a great leader. Instead, leadership abilities should depend on a person's strengths and personality traits (Martin, 2019). In many cases, women are not encouraged to pursue leadership roles as often as male counterparts, contributing to an imbalance in power (Martin, 2019).

According to Mohajan (2018) "Qualitative research is a form of social action that stresses on the way of people interpret and make sense of their experiences to understand the social reality of individuals" (p.2). Qualitative researchers seek to answer research questions through analysis (Adler, 1997). This qualitative study involved gathering information through interviews and analyzing participants' responses to determine the why, what, where, and how of the research. The study included 13 women between the ages of 30 and 65 who have held managerial or senior leadership positions within organizations. A sample size of 13 participants for interviews is suitable based on qualitative research standards described by Adu (2019) and Bloomberg and Volpe (2019). Many believe women's underrepresentation as leaders in organizations is because something or someone is holding women back from becoming leaders (Adler, 1997). This phenomenon is known as the glass ceiling effect, which is a barrier to women's advancement from middle-level management positions into leadership roles (Adler, 1997). Bias against women is subtle, and discrimination against women in the workplace, although illegal, remains an issue (Hill, 2016).

Berg and Lune's (2012) argued:

Quantitative measures appear objective, but only so long as we don't ask questions about where and how the data were produced; pure objectivity is not a meaningful concept if the goal is to measure intangibles [as] these concepts only exist because we can interpret them. (p. 340)

There are disadvantages to applying a quantitative research approach to a study (Creswell & Poth, 2018). Researchers applying a quantitative approach seek answers to specific questions so a particular hypothesis can be proven or disproven (Berg & Lune, 2012).

Quantitative research does not factor in people's motives when sharing an opinion (Creswell & Clark, 2018). The information-collecting process serves to paint a present-time picture of what is happening in the selected demographic (Creswell & Clark, 2018). However, the option cannot measure how society changes or how people interpret actions (Creswell & Clark, 2018). Quantitative research does not give one the option to review participants' responses (Berg & Lune, 2012). The quantitative option has very few opportunities to ask for clarity (Berg & Lune, 2012). Part of this disadvantage is the anonymous nature of the data researchers collect (Berg & Lune, 2012). If an answer provides inconclusive results, there is no way to guarantee the validity of what was received (Berg & Lune, 2012). It is even possible to skew results when a question might be incorrectly formatted (Berg & Lune, 2012). Finally, quantitative research methodology does not engage the respondents' experiences and perspectives in a controlled setting due to lacking a connection between researchers and the subjects when collecting data (Creswell & Creswell, 2018).

Weaknesses exist in mixed method design (Dodgson, 2019). First, the mixed method of research is more expensive and time-consuming than any other research method due to its duplicitous content (Liamputtong, 2019). Second, the study must be able to master several techniques, in tandem, with an ability to mix each method effectively (Dodgson, 2019). Similarly, many researchers believe that one should work within either qualitative or quantitative methods (Liamputtong, 2019). Finally, since it is a mixture of two relatively different research methods, many researchers and methodologists have yet to fully work out problems of interpreting conflicting results, quantitative data, and paradigm mixing (Liamputtong, 2019).

Other research designs such as case studies, grounded theory, or ethnography may also have been appropriate for this study, yet were not employed. Single case study analysis has been subject to several criticisms, the most common of which is that it lacks the inter-related issues of methodological rigor, researcher subjectivity, and external validity (Bloomberg & Volpe, 2019). Harvey and Brecher (2002) noted that the prototypical view suggests that "the use of the case study absolves the author from any kind of methodological considerations. Case studies have become in many cases a synonym for freeform research where anything goes" (Harvey & Brecher, 2002, pp. 164–165). The absence of systematic procedures for case study research is something that Bloomberg and Volpe (2019) perceived as traditionally the most significant concern due to a relative lack of methodological guidelines.

An issue with the grounded theory is that researchers will not know the extent of what they are studying until significant analysis has been completed (Clarke, 2005). The core category is the concept to which all other concepts relate, and its discovery signals the end of the open coding stage (Clarke, 2005). The grounded theory method takes various forms, which appear to be partly in contradiction, or even in dispute, with each other (Clarke, 2005). Ethnography was not selected because it is a time-consuming process. It takes time to build trust with participants to facilitate full and honest discourse (Adu, 2019). Short-term studies are at a particular disadvantage in this regard (Adu, 2019).

A qualitative phenomenological design allowed the study to analyze the data collected and interpreted (Glaser, 1978). The investigated the judgments that impact women's promotional status to leadership roles. The study used structured questions to gather ideas and insights from participants to identify the causes of women's underrepresentation in leadership. An analysis of the results helped determine the possible leading causes of women's underrepresentation in leadership roles (Glaser, 1978).

Conceptual Framework

A conceptual framework addresses the research problem and questions (Green, 2014). Conceptual frameworks are products of qualitative theorization processes (Jabareen, 2009). With conceptual frameworks, the research should first define "concept" and "conceptual framework" and then outline the processes and procedures of conceptual framework building (Jabareen, 2009, p. 57).

In this study, the conceptual framework was used to explore the challenges women face obtaining leadership positions (Green, 2014). A review of role congruity theory and transformational theory for women in leadership positions supported this approach. All of these theories provided a foundation for this research study.

Role congruity theory of prejudice toward female leaders expanded Eagly's (1987) research on role theory in sociologic terms (as cited in Eagly & Karau, 2002). Proponents of role congruity theory propose that a group positively evaluates when its characteristics align with its typical social roles (Dovidio et al., 2005). Coined by Eagly and Karau (2002), female leaders' prejudice occurs because inconsistencies exist between the characteristics of the female gender stereotype and those associated with the typical leadership. According to role congruity theorists, women are less likely than men to emerge as leaders when expectations for a leadership role are incongruent with gender stereotypes (Creswell & Creswell, 2018). Role congruity was suitable for this qualitative study, involving an attempt to determine factors that lead to denials of promotion for deserving women.

Burns (1978) created transformational leadership as a description of political leaders who transformed followers' values. Bass (1985, 1990) later expanded the scope to include leadership within organizational settings. Since then, transformational leadership has become one of the most widely studied leadership styles due to its emphasis on changing workplace norms and motivating employees to perform beyond expectations (Esser et al., 2018).

Transformational leadership theorists propose that leadership's definition presents a bias in favor of men as leaders and unfavorably toward women as leaders (Eagly & Karau, 2002;

McCleskey, 2014). The transformational leadership style is highly effective, using constructive mediating effects on change management (Kray et al., 2017) Transformational leadership style positively impacts organizational commitment (Singh & Vanka, 2020). Research findings on project managers and their leadership styles revealed that the participants' positions and the industry leaders work affected leadership styles (Robinson et al., 2017).

Warner et al. (2018) noted that, in the late 20th century, women made more rapid advances in the private sector than in the public sector. Simultaneously, the gender wage gap steadily decreased, gender segregation in most professions declined, and the percentage of women attaining management ranks rose (Warner et al., 2018). In 1980, there were no women in the top executive ranks of Fortune 100 companies (Warner et al., 2018).

There have long been significant racial and ethnic differences in women's advancement rate (Warner et al., 2018). Warner et al. (2018) noted that women of color comprised 39% of the nation's female population and 20% of the entire U.S. population. Also, women of color constitute 38.2% of the female civilian labor force, 18.2% of the total civilian labor force, and 18.5% of Standard and Poor's (S&P) 500 companies (Warner et al., 2018). Job performance, family views, political views, and salaries of women also served as a foundation for this study (Warner et al., 2018). An expanded discussion of the conceptual framework appears in the literature review in Chapter 2.

Definitions of Terms

- *Barriers*: Something immaterial that impedes or separates (Merriam-Webster Dictionary, 2021).
- *Bias:* A particular tendency, trend, inclination, feeling, or opinion, especially one that is preconceived or unreasoned (Dictionary.com, 2021).

- *C-Suite Leadership*: C-level executives play a strategic role within an organization; persons hold senior positions and impact company-wide decisions. C stands for *Chief*, so a C-level executive (also called a C-suite executive) is in charge of an entire department or business unit, such as marketing, finance, and IT (Pavlou, 2019).
- *Gender*: Refers to the characteristics of women, men, girls, and boys that are socially constructed. This includes norms, behaviors and roles associated with being a woman, man, girl, or boy, as well as relationships with each other. (World Health Organization, 2019).
- *Leadership*: The capacity of a company's management to set and achieve challenging goals, take fast and decisive action when needed, outperform the competition, and inspire others to perform at the highest level possible (Twin, 2020).
- *Mission*: The organization's or team's predefined purpose or reason for being (Society for Human Resource Management, 2020).
- *Phenomenology*: A philosophy initiated by Edmund Husserl (Gutland, 2018) at the beginning of the twentieth century. One key aim of phenomenology was to radically ground the foundation of knowledge so that skeptical attacks on rationality and its procedures could be overcome (Smith, 2003). A phenomenological researcher examines the qualities or essence of an experience through interviews, stories, or observations with people who have the experience of the researcher's interest (Connelly, 2010).
- *Role Congruity Theory:* A theory of prejudice toward female leaders that perceived incongruity between the female gender role and leadership roles leads to 2 forms of prejudice: (a) perceiving women less favorably than men as potential occupants of

leadership roles and (b) evaluating behavior that fulfills the prescriptions of a leader role less favorably when it is enacted by a woman (Eagly & Karau, 2002).

- *Transformational leadership*: The process by which a leader fosters group or organizational performance beyond expectation by virtue of the strong emotional attachment with his or her followers combined with the collective commitment to a higher moral cause (Bryman et al., 2011, p. 299).
- *Underrepresentation*: Inadequately represented (Merriam-Webster Dictionary, 2021).

Limitations and Delimitations

The aspects over which the researcher has no control are referred to as limitations (Bloomberg and Volpe, 2019). In most cases, each assumption you make becomes a limitation. The researcher's restrictions are the factors over which they have control. Delimitations are the qualities used by the researcher to define the study's bounds (Bloomberg and Volpe, 2019). The researcher takes deliberate exclusionary and inclusionary judgments on the sample, the variables researched theoretical views, tools, and generalizability (Simon, 2011).

Limitations

According Simon (2011), limitations are "potential weaknesses in your study and are out of your control" (p. 1). Bloomberg and Volpe (2019) noted that "limitations of the study are those characteristics of design or methodology that impacted or influenced the interpretation of the findings, from the research" (p. 207). Every research has its limitations. These limitations can appear due to constraints on methodology or research design. Stating the limitations of a study may impact the researcher's entire study. However, when a researcher acknowledges the study's limitations, it demonstrates that all sides of the study have been explored. As a result, mentioning the limitations demonstrates honesty and integrity, as well as a thorough comprehension of the subject.

Delimitations

According to Bloomberg and Volpe (2019), delimitations refer to the original decisions made concerning the general design of a study and should not be confused with reporting the limitations of the study that were identified after the research was done. According to Simon (2011), delimitations are "those characteristics that limit the scope and define the boundaries of your study and are within the researcher's control" (p. 2). There is no study that is perfect or covers every potential angle. Participant exclusion criteria are a clear example of a delimitation that applies to practically every research project. In order to perform a quantitative or qualitative study, the researcher must first determine the population of interest. Defining this demographic of interest necessitates the researcher articulating the boundaries of that population. Those lines represent delimitations.

This qualitative study involved gathering responses from conducted interviews. The limited number of participants only provided data through their responses. The limited number of participants caused some difficulty identifying significant relationships from the data. The responses provided by the research participants proved to be a limiting factor (Delva et al., 2002). Another limitation was time. A study conducted over a specific time interval is only a snapshot dependent on conditions occurring during that time.

The factors that restrict the scope and characterize the limits of the study, such as the sample size, geographical area or environment in which the investigation takes place, demographic attributes, and so on, are referred to as delimitations (Sallis, 2021). In exploring a potential explanation for the imbalance of gender representation in leadership positions for women, the study's delimitations were affected by education, job performance, politics, salary, and family dynamics. The results of this study were generalizable to women who: (a) work in corporate positions, (b) work in the state of South Carolina, and (c) have more than ten years of leadership experience.

This study investigated the self-reported leadership behavior of female leaders in the context of women who achieve fewer leadership roles than men, regardless of education, job performance, political views, salary, and family dynamics. Research does not indicate how many more men hold leadership positions than women (Tabassum & Nayak, 2021). Various factors may contribute to the underrepresentation of women in leadership positions (Delva et al., 2002). The study involved interviewing women who have worked in hierarchical companies for at least 10 years. The interviews consisted of women who have worked alongside men whose qualifications matched or exceeded their male-counterparts and have proven to be strong leaders who have not achieved promotions in their organization's leadership positions. The responses were based on the participants' perceptions of their own leadership experiences and cannot be verified by others to determine if the participants' leadership perceptions were aligned with how others perceived the participants' leadership capabilities.

Also, these leaders were from various geographic regions. The leaders interviewed came from different family dynamics, social and cultural backgrounds, and held different perceptions. Lastly, only leaders from medium to large scale organizations participated in this study, therefore responses do not represent all corporation sizes.

The objective was to obtain in-depth information from interviews. The information gained from this study will contribute to the knowledge base of women leaders in medium to large organizations by providing insight into how these women experience and demonstrate overcoming rising leadership challenges. Because this is a qualitative study, the ability to generalize the findings was not a goal. The locations, selected samples, and specific components of the organizations explored limited the study's scope.

Chapter Summary

This chapter included an introduction to the qualitative phenomenological research study on investigating the factors that may cause the underrepresentation of women in leadership positions. This chapter shared background information regarding the underrepresentation of women in leadership roles through related research. In the problem and purpose statements outlined the issues associated with women not achieving leadership positions for which they are qualified. Discussion included the strategy to interview successful women and to determine the appropriate sample size to complete the study. Education level, job performance, political views, salaries, and family values served as a foundation for this study. The study analyzed the ideas, feelings, and individual experiences the participants may experience when denied the opportunity to obtain a leadership position. Chapter 1 also outlined a research assumption, the conceptual framework, the limitations, and the study's delimitations.

Chapter 2 includes a literature review to provide a historical perspective on women in leadership. The literature review builds a conceptual framework to better understand the feelings and desires of women who wish to be part of a leadership team. Chapter 2 includes a review of the educational levels, job performance, political views, salaries, and family values of women to conceptualize and analyze women's underrepresentation in leadership.

CHAPTER 2: LITERATURE REVIEW

The current literature regarding feminism includes several approaches to examining the differences between men and women in addressing equality and opportunity (Painter-Morland & Werhane, 2011). In the sphere of leadership, the equality debate has frequently challenged women with the task of simply doing what men have always been able to do, but better (Painter-Morland & Werhane, 2011). As a result, unintentionally, female pioneers have maintained male leadership preconceptions (Tucker, 2018). However, there is more conversation on how women may be better incorporated in leadership positions (Ely & Padavic, 2020). Demonstrating this is one of the through this doctoral study.

Barriers and biases contributing to the scarcity of senior female leadership in governmental organizations and private industries across the United States remain unknown. To investigate this phenomenon, the literature used in this research was immense and comprehensive. Reviewing materials from web-based searches to book reviews, this study cites 228 references, 76% (173) of which came from articles, 1% (2) of the referenced information came from dissertations, and 23% (53) of the cited resources were drawn from published books. With a publishing date of 2022, 38% (86) of the referenced material spanned from 2016 and prior. The balance, 62% (142) of the referenced material spanned from 2017 and after. Key research terms for this research include: women, executive leadership, gender-biases, gender discrimination, and equality.

The literature on leadership theory offers some foresight into gender and leadership roles. Just as leadership definitions continue to evolve, gender fits into leadership styles, and characteristics account for much research on gender and leadership (Ely et al., 2011; Verniers & Vala, 2018; Weinberg et al., 2019). Because cultural beliefs shape leadership definitions and what it means to be a leader, contemporary researchers consider leadership characteristics assigned to gender roles and society's perceptions of gender in leadership roles (Chanland & Murphy, 2018; Weinberg et al., 2019). According to Travis and Thorpe-Moscon (2018), courage and certainty have typically been accepted as characteristics indicative of male leadership. Challenging this conventional view, Parker et al. (2017) contended that the consistent phenomenon of the lack of gender diversity in organizational leadership is due to societal perception that women lack leadership capabilities.

Societal expectations remain steadfast concerning how males and females should behave in leadership roles (Eagly & Carli, 2007; Kalaitzi et al., 2017). Therefore, a likely cause of gender discrimination is the conflict that arises from leadership traits described as communal, agentic, or non-gendered (Ben-Noam, 2018 ; Eagly & Carli, 2007). National Academies of Sciences, Engineering, and Medicine (2018) stated that women are identified as possessing virtues such as thoughtfulness, politeness, and sympathy. Ali (2018) stated that men and women are innately assigned various characteristics. Men and women can be similarly known for insightfulness and charm, but possessing more assertive and supercilious characteristics is quintessentially correlated with a male gender role (Brock & Ma, 2021).

According to Shriver (2009), nearly half of professionals in the U.S. are women. Additionally, women are either the primary providers or co-providers in almost two-thirds of American families (Shriver, 2009). There are varying circumstances when the breadwinner or co-breadwinner of a family prioritizes family obligations over career advancement. According to Ely and Rhode (2010), "Many of the women who step off the leadership track are not entirely happy with the decision" (p. 389). In 2007, census data indicated that 80% of mothers in the U.S. were employed (Cotter et al., 2007). According to Ellison (2005), "The 2000 U.S. Census found a record 10 million single mothers living with children younger than eighteen, up from 3 million in 1970—implying a greater financial responsibility for mothers than ever before" (p. 177). Women earned 59% of all degrees for postsecondary education in 2008 (Ely & Rhode, 2010). Studies have shown that American women are increasingly outnumbering male students in universities across the nation; however, females are only out-earning male counterparts in a small number of cities (Leonhardt, 2008). Leonhardt (2008) asserted:

> Armed with college degrees, large numbers of women have entered fields once dominated by men. Nearly half of new doctors today are women, up from just 1 of every 10 in the early 1970s. In all, the average inflation-adjusted weekly pay of women has jumped [26%] since 1980. (para. 11)

Barriers to Advancement

Women are not entering executive-level positions at the same rate as male counterparts, even though women are as educated and trained and hired by organizations at the same rate (Davidson & Burke, 2004). Rodriguez and Giuffrida (2019) examined the relationship between gender attitudes, curriculum choices, education levels, occupational aspirations, and college students' expectations. The authors found that gender ideology is related to women's career ambition in gender study areas (Weber & Cissna-Heath, 2016). Since gender ideology influences young women's educational and occupational expectations, regardless of social background, at least some gender segregation within all career lines may be due to the gender values women bring into the labor market (Weber & Cissna-Heath, 2016). Scant women have climbed to the highest corporate levels, and in 1997, only 3% of top executives in America's top 500 companies were women (Weber & Cissna-Heath, 2016). Since that time, there has been little progress, and women are not advancing to organizations' upper levels at the same rate as men (Davidson & Burke, 2004).

In 1869, Galson proposed one of the earliest leadership ideas known as the great man theory (GMT) (McCleskey, 2014). Citing GMT, McCleskey (2014) postulated that only a man could have significant leader characteristics. In GMT, persons are born with specific characteristics and traits not commonly found in the majority of the population (McCleskey, 2014). Yet, when found, the markers are predominantly found in men (McCleskey, 2014). In GMT, the skills and attributes of leadership are not learned but somewhat inherent to one's character ((Dyczkowska & Dyczkowski, 2018). Similarly, research on gender and leadership has generally focused on the glass ceiling notion (Dyczkowska & Dyczkowski, 2018). Women face the challenge of societal perceptions of male leadership characteristics (Goulart et al., 2021). Although current research indicates that women can lead effectively, stereotypes and challenges exist that may impede female leaders' success (Goulart et al., 2021). Gender discrimination is perpetual and continues to hinder women's advancement (Goulart et al., 2021). In a study examining theories of prejudice toward women, Eagly and Karau (2002) found that women emerge less commonly than men as leaders because women have to meet a higher standard than men due to men already being considered highly competent.

Another challenge American women face is in the political arena (Brechenmaker, 2018). According to Brechenmaker (2018), politics are partly structural. Because of its single-member congressional districts, the United States has historically lagged behind other countries in terms of women's representation (Brechenmaker, 2018). In 2019, women constituted 23.7% of Congress, which exceeds the current global average of 24% (Sanbonmatsu, 2020).

According to Horowitz et al.'s (2018a) research from the Pew Research Center, the partisan gap in female leaders' numbers is even more comprehensive than the gender gap. According to the same study by Horowitz et al. (2018a),

> Democrats and Democratic-leaning independents are more than twice as likely as Republicans and those who lean Republican to say there are too few women in high political offices (79% vs. 33%). And while 64% of Democrats say gender discrimination is a significant reason woman are underrepresented in these positions, only 30% of Republicans agree. (para. 2)

Yet, Devex (2020) shared a compelling argument that countries with a more significant proportion of women as top decision-makers in legislatures have lower income inequality levels. Rogers (2021) stated,

> The United States sent a historically senior and diverse delegation to the 65th session of the Commission on the Status of Women, where Vice President Kamala Harris delivered an address to the United Nations last week — making her the highest-ranking U.S. government official ever to do so at the event. (para. 1)

And during her speech to the United Nations, Vice President Harris "used the opportunity to confirm the United States' commitment to women's rights on the world stage" (2021, para. 1). Vice President Harris' remarks reiterated the sentiments of Devex argument on the importance of having women in top-leadership positions.

Companies in the top-quartile for gender diversity on executive teams are 21% more likely to outperform the national average (Devex, 2020). Yet, leadership has been predominantly a male prerogative in corporate, political, military, and other social sectors (Eagly & Karau, 2002). The public and scientific discussion has centered on the idea of a *glass ceiling*, a barrier of prejudice and discrimination that excludes women from higher-level leadership positions (U.S. Department of Labor, 1995). Prejudice toward female leaders follows from the incongruity that many people perceive between women's characteristics and the leader role requirements (Eagly & Karau, 2002). Research thus suggests more constancy in the stereotypes that people hold about women and men than the stereotypes people have about leaders. Individual differences in social perceivers may also influence the incongruity between leader and gender roles (Eagly & Karau, 2002).

One such variable is perceivers' gender, given evidence that men often have a more masculine construal of leadership than women (Eagly & Karau, 2002). Proof of this construal emerges mainly from studies on perceptions of the managerial role similar to Schein's (1984). According to Eagly and Karau's (2002) review of research, more recent studies have shown that in the United States, women, as compared with men, generally have a more androgynous view of managerial roles as requiring communal qualities as well as agentic ones. This difference between men and women managers' perception likely reflects women's considerably greater experience with female managers (Eagly & Karau, 2002). Over the past few years, there have been numerous studies regarding the leadership concept (Alvinius, 2017). According to Alvinius (2017), the leadership concept analyzed alongside gender characteristics further reveals some exciting tendencies in the future of the business world.

Organizational Culture

A 2016 American Association of University Women (AAUW) report indicated the lack of women in leadership roles can be examined through structural barriers preventing women's ascent to leadership and the gender bias that continues to impact women in the workplace. According to AAUW (2016), in changing workplace culture to address the lack of women in leadership, specific issues differ depending on location. Although more women are educated in the U.S. than are men, and women constitute nearly half of the workforce, women are promoted at work far less often than men (AAUW, 2016). Women make up less than 5% of CEOs, and less than 10% of women are top earners in the Standard and Poor's (S&P) 500 (Wilson, 2019). Women of color are more disadvantaged than other ethnicities, as women of color are nearly invisible on both S&P 500 boards and Fortune 500 boards (Wilson, 2019).

Gender bias plays a role in gender discrepancy at executive levels in organizations across the United States, although women hold 51% of all middle management positions (Bertrand et al., 2019). According to Bertrand et al. (2019), female middle managers may be overlooked for advancement to executive positions because of a lack of synergy between individual career planning and organizational development and advancement practices. Significant implications may result for organizations as they struggle to recruit and hire qualified senior leadership to close the widening gap created as baby boomers leave the workforce in record numbers over the next decade (Bertrand et al., 2019). One way to retain talented and knowledgeable female middle managers is to incorporate career planning and advancement programs, which increases visibility for both the individual and organizational leaders regarding potential advancement opportunities (Schulz & Enslin, 2014).

In general, women are underrepresented in most leadership positions (Schulz & Enslin, 2014). This underrepresentation is more customary in Black women (Schulz & Enslin, 2014). According to Schulz and Enslin (2014), Black women must often prove capability in leadership positions, and if they are fortunate enough to land leadership positions, proficiency of their work is scrutinized. Black women must go the extra mile to prove they are proficient and worthy of the position—obstacles that male counterparts, overall, do not have to face (Acosta & Carpenter, 2014).

One of these obstacles is known as the glass ceiling effect, which is a concept that represents invisible barriers faced by women and minorities when attempting to secure executing leadership positions, regardless of qualifications and education (Bertrand et al., 2019). There is a common thread in research that puts White men at the forefront of nearly every athletic position in intercollegiate sports, such as coaches and athletic directors (Acosta & Carpenter, 2014). Therefore, White men continue to hire other White men, perpetuating the discrimination against any other race and gender (Acosta & Carpenter, 2014).

According to Kray et al. (2017), men are considered masculine role models who offer organizational success, while women are classified as meek and compassionate and excellent at fulfilling relationship-oriented roles. Because of these adopted stereotypes, women who assert and attempt to land leadership positions are repeatedly met with resistance and continue to face challenges that male counterparts often escape (Gumbs, 2018). This leads to Black women striving to be heard, which often is depicted as misplaced anger and overreacting to specific social issues (Dickens et al., 2019).

Discrimination in Economic Systems

The highest-paid administrators at the top of corporations are the president, chief operating officer, chief executive officer, and chairman (Davidson & Burke, 2004). Only two women held any of these posts in the United States in the 1970s, and by 2007, women held only 6% of these positions. (Eagly & Carli, 2007). Men, who account for more than three-quarters of American workers earning $100,000–$200,000, are generally awarded the highest-paying jobs (Pritlove et al., 2019). Only 56 women are among the 400 wealthiest Americans (Shapiro, 2020).

Women are recognized to perform better than men in general, according to Warner et al. (2018), and gender does not appear to impact a woman's ability to lead. Since 1988, women have outnumbered men on college campuses (Warner et al., 2018). Women have received at least one-third of legal degrees since 1980 and one-third of medical school students by 1990, although they have not risen to positions of prominence and influence in America (Warner et al., 2018). In many industries, women's representation in top leadership positions such as law partners, medical school deans, and business executive officers remains frozen at 5 percent to 20%. (Warner et al., 2018). Overall, there is a vast disparity between a tiny number of influential women at the top of their sectors and the great majority of women across the country (Warner et al., 2018). The gap between American women and their counterparts in other countries is widening (Warner et al., 2018).

Researchers have investigated the factors that contribute to the failure of closing the gap despite regulations designed to prevent inequity from occurring (Wynen et al., 2015). Women who work in a male-dominated industry are likely to earn less than male counterparts are and less likely to be promoted (Lopez & Ensari, 2014). Women appear to get jobs that have a gender-bias making this this type of segregation in the workplace is called occupational segregation (Lopez & Ensari, 2014). According to Hegewisch and Liepmann (2013), occupational segregation causes gender inequality in the workplace, including a pay inequity. Because of this segregation, more women have been employed as secretaries, nurses, and schoolteachers, whereas more men are in computer sciences, engineering, and business occupations (Bolitzer & Godtland, 2012).

Occupational segregation by race is not as pronounced as occupational segregation by gender and has declined considerably since 1940 (Xu & Leffler, 1992). According to Xu and

Leffler (1992), "Gender outweighs race as a determinant of labor force concentration, although both gender and race effect occupational distributions" (Xu & Leffler, 1992, p. 382). While occupational segregation by gender limits all women's employment options, "racial and ethnic segmentation within typical women's jobs further constrains the employment options of women of color" (Segura, 1989, p. 38). The number of working women did increase during the Great Depression, while many men were unemployed (Rodriguez & Giuffrida, 2019). Social policies in the 1930s supported men being paid more than women through a family wage, which rested on the assumption that families were not relying on the female for economic provision (Hattery, 2001). The American economy relied on women to join the labor force during World War II, while men served in the armed services (Hattery, 2001). In 1940, female workers increased to 25% of the workforce (Hattery, 2001). Policies improved throughout the 1940s, which prohibited wage discrimination based on direct favoritism towards men (Reid et al., 2018). And before the Second Industrial Revolution, the manufacturing industry was in full swing (Kinyanjui, 2021).

Despite these developments, the wage gap between men and women still expands due to job segregation by gender (Manzi, 2019). This has been called the gender division of labor or the delegation of tasks according to a person's gender (Hoobler et al., 2018). Societies delegate tasks in part based on workers' gender, although the duties vary over time and across countries (Hoobler et al., 2018). Family wages were associated with jobs for men and individual wages for women (Kinyanjui, 2021). Women's roles in the United States have shifted over time as roles within the family, and the changing nature of employment has evolved. Historical context frames how women's roles are perceived (Kinyanjui, 2021).

Researchers have examined gender discrimination in wages and promotion to determine whether or not the returns for skills and job characteristics are more significant for one gender than the other once other determinants of wages are taken into account (Tucker, 2018). Although these methods are generally accepted, organizations are vulnerable to omitting wages that may explain gender differentials, including determinants biased by prior gender discrimination (Tucker, 2018). Despite these ambiguities, there is general agreement that such studies have demonstrated wage discrimination against women (Tucker, 2018). However, Hoobler et al.'s (2017) meta-analysis of the results of 41 studies estimating wage discrimination indicated an unequivocal decrease over time. Other detailed analyses indicated that some wage discrimination against women remains in the United States (Tabassum & Nayak, 2021).

According to Kennedy (2018), there is still a rather large wage gap between women and men in the American workforce. Devillard et al. (2019) suggested that sexism and discrimination play a significant role in the cause of the wage disparity gap experienced by women in organizations, and a consequence of the disparity is that women are settling for a lower wage (Devillard et al., 2019). The highest paid jobs typically go to men, and men have more continuity in careers while women have to opt-out to have families or change companies to progress (Forbes Coaches Council, 2018).

Researchers have investigated factors that contribute to the failure of closing the gap despite legislation designed to prevent inequity from occurring (Wynen et al., 2015). Many researchers have studied why pay injustice occurs, factors contributing to gender stereotyping, and occupational segregation (Bolitzer & Godtland, 2012). Women who work in a male-dominated industry are less likely to be promoted and earn less than their male counterparts (Lopez & Ensari, 2014). Wynen et al. (2015) believed occupational segregation occurs in patterns, horizontally and vertically. Women are striving to keep paychecks and satisfying employment while maintaining a complete family life, as well (Ammerman & Groysberg, 2021). Although women can now hold almost any job, the tensions of trying to raise a family and hold simultaneously maintain employment are still high (Dickens et al., 2019).

Large numbers of women have worked lower-paid jobs such as waitresses, secretaries, cashiers, elementary school teachers, and childcare workers, explaining this historic wage gap (Selzer et al., 2017). Babcock et al. (2021) blamed the discrepancy in pay on women not asking for higher salaries. Yet, sexism and discrimination also play a prominent role in the cause of this gap (Babcock et al., 2021). It has become a self-fulfilling prophecy to some degree, and women are settling for a lower wage (Devillard et al., 2019). According to Miller (2016), the highest paid jobs typically have more continuity in careers, while some women have had to change companies for promotions. In societies that devalue women's work, women's pay is lower than men's compensation (Tabassum & Nayak, 2021). Thorne (2020) suggested that the wage gap is related to the fact that men rise in rank higher than women because they have more mentors than women.

There is a need for an appraisal and compensation system that is uniform for men and women to ensure that women are not paid less for the same jobs (Chanland & Murphy, 2018). According to Devillard et al. (2019), workplace policies make a difference in employee retention, and this is a political strategy that may ensure assistance for women who strive for work-life balance. According to Fields and Wolff (1991), female workers' wages differ significantly by industry, even when the analysis controls workers' productivity-related characteristics. Of the overall gender wage gap, the average female worker earns about 65% as much as the average male worker (Fields & Wolff, 1991). Between 12%–22% of this disparity is based on the differences between the patterns of inter-industry wage differentials of men and women and 15%–19% by differences in male and female workers' distribution across industries

(Fields & Wolff, 1991). However, discrimination against women regarding pay and promotion exists today in a lesser sense than it did in the past (Devillard et al., 2019).

Nevertheless, evidence indicates an inequity still exists amongst women compared to male counterparts (Ammerman & Groysberg, 2021). Although the salary gap has lessened over the years, decreasing from 42% in 1960 to 21% gap in 2014, more than 40 years is projected to pass before women's payment is expected to be equal to men (Graf et al., 2019). While gender equality policies are generally in place, not all policies are adequately implemented, and there is often an inherent bias in recruitment, selection, and promotion (Alvinius, 2017).

Horowitz et al. (2018b) indicated that uneven expectations and companies not being ready to elevate women are cited more than any other factor as a primary reason why more women are not in top leadership roles in business. Approximately employees in four out of ten businesses claim that women are held to higher expectations than men (Horowitz et al., 2018a). Many businesses are also hesitant to recruit women for senior executive roles (Chira, 2017). Six out of 10 women believe that having to justify competencies more than men is a major cause for women's underrepresentation in high-level government roles (61%) and top executive positions in industry (60 %) (Horowitz et al., 2018b).

Women face two types of structural issues: (a) some are found in society, and (b) others are found in corporate settings (Brock & Ma, 2021). Societal problems are those forces that are deeply rooted in culture and public policy (Brock & Ma, 2021). Contributing factors to the limited career advancement for women include some aspects of social programs and policy, fixed human capital, and the societal expectation of female participation in service industries such as education, health services, and social and community services (Smith et al., 2019). Social policy directed toward women perpetuates inequality in domestic obligations (Smith et al.,

2019). When maternity leaves are favored over paternity leaves, or when women are encouraged to work part-time after a child's birth, men are not afforded equal opportunity to do so (Smith et al., 2019). According to Smith et al. (2019), the social perception is that it is more appropriate for women to fulfill the commitment regarding family responsibilities than men.

Studies have indicated that leadership impacts the culture of an organization (Schein, 1984). The leader's management style and beliefs influence its culture (Schein, 1984). Various authors have studied the differences between men and women leaders, but less so on the impact of a leader's traits on an organization's culture (Warner & Corley, 2017). Decades after the feminist revolution, women are still struggling to be seen as leaders within organizations, even though many have implemented hiring and recruitment policies to help eliminate this problem (Walker & Aritz, 2015, p. 460).

Human capital refers to the skills, experience, and knowledge an employee brings to a position (Esser et al., 2018). Cultural expectations deem it more appropriate for women to interrupt careers due to family responsibilities, such as caring for children or aging parents, than for men to do the same (Hall, 2018). Moreover, women are encouraged to work in departments with fewer developmental opportunities or those that do not translate to executive advancement (Hoobler et al., 2018). Longman et al. (2018) noted that women in management are more likely to come from non-business backgrounds, limiting attempts to succeed because women have little or no business leadership experience. The phenomenon of *glass cliffs* is another threat to women entering power positions. This scenarios occurs when women are favored for jobs that lead units in crisis, creating a scenario in which burnout or failure is a potential risk (Warner & Corley, 2017).

Occupational Segregation

According to Tariq and Syed (2017), women are underrepresented in labor force upper leadership within business organizations. Women are now entering the workforce faster than men; however, women are underrepresented in leadership positions across nearly all industries (Tariq & Syed, 2017). Women make up only 2% of chief executive officers (CEOs), 14% of top executives, and 16% of directors at Fortune 500 companies (Rule & Ambady, 2009). It is evident from this assessment that women are barely present in upper leadership (Rule & Ambady, 2009). Even though women represent the majority of the workforce, they continue to face significant barriers when climbing the corporate ladder (Eagly & Carli, 2007).

According to the Washington Center for Equitable Growth (2017), occupational segregation occurs in employment when one demographic group is either overrepresented or underrepresented. The evidence shows that occupational segregation based on gender occurs more because of assumptions about the kind of work different genders are best suited for than because of an efficient allocation of innate talent (Washington Center for Equitable Growth, 2017). Furthermore, data show that overrepresentation of disadvantaged groups of workers in occupations lowers pay regardless of other productivity metrics such as necessary skill level, and that integration across occupations has stagnated for Black and Latinx employees (Monroe, 2020).

Men are compensated at a higher rate regardless of skillset or education level (Eagly & Carli, 2007). If work is done predominantly by women, it is valued less in the labor market (Washington Center for Equitable Growth, 2017). As the rate of women working in a given occupation increases, the pay in that occupation declines even when controlling for education and skills (Washington Center for Equitable Growth, 2017). According to the Washington Center for Equitable Growth (2017), many careers that will add the most jobs by 2024, including health care support, administrative assistance, early childhood care, education, and food preparation and services, are composed of more than 60% women.

Role Congruity Theory

Another barrier, and perhaps the most significant to women, is that the "old-boy network" excludes women from top management (Goethals et al., 2011, p. 79). Goethals et al. (2011) stated that the old-boy network consists of males educated at the same institutions who climbed the corporate ladder together. Goethals et al. reported the lack of women in high-level executive leadership roles is principally due to an innate bias against women as leaders when taking all evidence from research into consideration. In these top decision-making roles, men often seek out former colleagues and friends to fill these positions (Goethals et al., 2011). According to Goethals et al. many corporations claim to be meritocracies, and advancement is determined by performance and skill. Despite many men and women's similar educational attainments, ambitions, status, starting salaries, and commitments to careers, men generally progress faster and attain higher-status positions, receiving significantly higher compensation than women. Goethals et al. suggested that men's associations play a significant role in rise to power and prestige.

According to Heilman (2012), stereotyping is, in part, generalizing behavioral characteristics of groups of people and then applying the generalization to individuals who are members of the group. Researchers recently investigated gender stereotyping by dividing the conceptions into two properties, descriptive and prescriptive (Heilman, 2012). Heilman (2012) focused on the significances of each of those properties. Descriptive stereotyping describes how women and men are alike, and prescriptive stereotyping define how men and women should be

(Ely et al., 2011). For example, descriptive stereotyping toward women created negative expectations about a woman's performance as a leader because there is a lack of fit between the roles assigned to women and the characteristics assigned to traditional male leadership roles (Heilman, 2012). Prescriptive stereotypes, or ascribing behaviors to what women should be like and the agentic elements of leadership, creates an incongruity with expected female behavior (Ely et al., 2011; Weinberg et al., 2019; Wynen et al., 2015;). Heilman (2012) further argued that whether or not gender stereotyping is descriptive or prescriptive, the practice impedes women's progress into leadership roles.

Descriptive and prescriptive gender stereotypes are a precursor to female leaders' prejudice and negative attitudes toward women in power positions (Heilman, 2012). When women are in top-level positions, the role congruity theory of bias toward a female leader remains for women once women attain these roles because performance evaluation is higher (Heilman, 2012). Researchers have found that women are viewed as less effective when performing in the more masculine leadership parts (Lopez & Ensari 2014). Eagly and Carli (2007) suggested that while praised for leadership-worthy skills, the fact that women remain behind men in attaining leadership positions remains an issue.

Although many women have proven to be influential leaders, a stereotypical view of women remains that focuses on the role congruity theory of prejudice toward women leaders (Eagly & Carli, 2007). The theoretical construct suggests that biases against women as leaders occur because of inconsistencies between leadership characteristics and the attributes of female gender stereotypes (Eagly & Carli, 2007). For example, assigning masculine characteristics to the definition of leadership styles creates an inconsistency with that role and the concept of feminine characteristics that society places on the female gender (Eagly & Carli, 2007). Female characteristics are incompatible with masculine characteristics that define leadership roles; therefore, there is a contradiction between accepting or perceiving women in a leadership role over men (Eagly & Carli, 2007).

Esser et al. (2018) described the roadblocks in ambitious women's career paths as external obstacles within organizations that prevent women's upward mobility. Common female roles, a scarcity of mentors and role models, poor standards of women's skills, and sexism in a predominantly male-dominated system are all obstacles to progression (Lopez & Ensari, 2014). According to Businesswire (2013),

> Only 38% of professional women think they will rise to a more senior leadership position in their companies. Those who do not cite lack of opportunities to be promoted (41%), reluctance to take time away from their families or personal lives (30%), and not being interested in staying at their companies long enough to advance (20%) as the top three reasons they are unlikely to advance (para. 5).

Yet, despite consistent growth, professional women say that women have the least influence over financial prospects and job success (Businesswire, 2013).

Research has continued to produce similar results over the past decades (Lennon et al., 2013). Lennon et al. (2013) reported that the lack of women in high-level executive leadership roles is principally due to an innate bias against women as leaders when taking all evidence from research into consideration. Selzer et al. (2017) reviewed a 2015 Pew Research study that found that 40% of those polled believe there is a double standard for women seeking executive positions in business. The research on role congruity theory places leadership gender bias within a perspective that theorizes bias as developing when stereotypical beliefs about specific social group behaviors are viewed as being incongruent with gender role (Eagly & Carli, 2007; Eagly

& Karau, 2002; Heilman, 2012). Lopez and Ensari (2014) found a connection between gender, leadership style, and organizational success. According to Lopez and Ensari, evidence of the role incongruity theory of prejudice was demonstrated when organizations, under the auspices of females with autocratic leadership styles, failed.

Gender equality is multidimensional and includes several dimensions of gender relations in the division of labor, emotions, symbolic representations, and power and decision-making (Enwemeka, 2018). Within an organization, these patterns of gender relations constitute a gender regime (Enwemeka, 2018). Gender regime can include inequalities between women and men in the shape of discrimination concerning opportunities, access to services, and allocation of resources or benefits (Enwemeka, 2018). According to Enwemeka (2018), these aspects of gender inequalities influence women's and men's working life and can lead to gendered experiences of somatic and mental health status. Gender inequalities are social obstacles that prevent fairness in health status between women and men, making it a significant public health issue (Enwemeka, 2018).

Women tend to work at lower hierarchical levels than men, and even within management, the upper echelons are held by men (Alqahtani, 2020). The higher the hierarchy is, the lower the women's share (Trzcinski & Holst, 2010). While women in management are less segregated than other female employees, the opposite is true for men (Busch & Holst, 2011). Managerial positions show gender-specific occupational differences in the enterprise's size, economy, and industry (Busch & Holst, 2011). Many researchers analyzed the effects of working in a gender-typical or atypical profession on wages and wage differentials between women and men (Busch & Holst, 2011). Worse employment conditions in wages generally characterize women's occupations (Busch & Holst, 2011). Women are often leaders of smaller firms and more frequently work in health care, welfare, and private services (Busch & Holst, 2011). Women with a university degree more often choose a field of study dominated by women, such as humanities (Busch & Holst, 2011). Also, there are more female managers in public services than in the private sector (Busch & Holst, 2011).

Gender inequality relates to unfairness and unequal access for both men and women (Sampson & Gresham, 2017). Most societies have gender inequities, and education has the most apparent gender inequity in leadership (Sampson & Gresham, 2017). Researchers suggested that more studies should be conducted on why women obtained the top position in specific companies' leadership (Sampson & Gresham, 2017). Gender inequity or inequality relates to women because women are often marginalized (Sampson & Gresham, 2017). Cook and Glass (2014) shared that research on women leaders often emphasized some women's success but rarely examined organizations or women in general as leaders.

Leadership Theory

Post (2017) opposed the stereotypical belief that women do not fit the preconceived notions of a leader, one of the many explanations offered for the lack of women in top leadership positions. Heilman (2012) argued that descriptive stereotyping toward women creates negative expectations about a woman's lack of fit in leadership roles because of the contradiction between the societal roles assigned to women and the characteristics assigned to traditional male leadership roles. Women executives are concentrated in specific areas, such as personnel, public relations, and even finance specialties, seldom leading to the most potent top management posts (Goethals et al. 2011).

The research on leadership theories relates to the literature on gender and leadership roles. Noting that solid leadership is associated with masculine gender role traits such as assertiveness, confidence, and control, UN Women (2020) stated that people have behavioral expectations for how men and women should behave socially. According to Ely et al. (2011), leadership in masculine terms uses the adjectives decisive, assertive, and healthy, in contrast to female qualities such as friendliness, caring, and community (Ely et al., 2011). Ely et al. found that women are stereotypically defined as passive, lacking ambition, or overemotional. While there are indeed women who have reached high management positions, women in leadership are often perceived, given their scarcity, as merely "tokens" (Ely et al., 2011, p. 480). Thus, corporate management cannot be accused of discrimination (Goethals et al., 2011).

Some theories are worthy of consideration when contemplating the reasons why women do not have a more significant presence in high-level leadership positions. One concept is the social role theory (Eagly, 1987). The social role's general premise is on roles as causes of behaviors enacted by individual groups and inferences about individuals or groups (Eagly, 1987). Eagly and Karau's (2002) role congruity theory of prejudice demonstrated a bias toward female leaders and leadership theory. McCleskey (2014) proposed that leadership's definition presents a tendency to favor men as leaders and unfavorably toward women as leaders. Many women believe they will have to give up aspects of their personal life if they want to attain success in the workforce (Brue, 2019). Many women in leadership positions insist that the most critical career strategy for advancing to senior levels is to exceed performance expectations consistently (Goethals et al., 2011). In other words, according to Goethals et al. (2011), for women to move up the corporate ladder, they must work harder and longer than male counterparts. Brue (2019) stated that as long as the culture continues to define careers as all-consuming, there may be no solution to the dilemma.

Gender Stereotypes in the Workplace

One cannot approach gender bias and stereotypical female behavior in the workplace without noting inequities (Wynen et al., 2015). The reason for this is that researchers often consider the inequality between the salaries of men and women (Wynen et al., 2015). Bolitzer and Godtland (2012) found that the pay gap is narrowing, but still exists. The authors noted that the difference in pay declined between 1988 and 2007 (Bolitzer & Godtland, 2012). One reason for the drop may be that men and women have become more alike in work experience and education levels (Bolitzer & Godtland, 2012). Lennon et al. (2013) reported that women are outperforming men but that salaries do not reflect that high performance. However, a gap remains. Bolitzer and Godtland expressed that if education and job experience are not attributed to the gap, then perhaps pay inequity is due to unequal treatment in the workforce.

The majority of women laboring in the largest and most unwavering U.S. companies work in jobs at the lower levels of organizational hierarchies (Cockburn, 1991). Research validates the lack of advancement opportunities in all types of female-dominated low-paying jobs (Cockburn, 1991). Beyond low-paying jobs, advancement must be considered in a broader context than mere movement up the hierarchy of a private sector firm or public sector agency (Cockburn, 1991). In the best case, advancement means a job change that results in better pay, benefits, working conditions, or security (Cockburn, 1991). The most significant gap is in power, prestige, and compensation and is more often awarded to people working at the top of organizations than those working at the bottom of or outside organizations, exacerbating the barriers to improving mobility for women (Cockburn, 1991). According to Cockburn (1991), improving women's advancement opportunities requires substantial restructuring in societal organizations.

A significant body of research indicates that for women, the subtle gender bias that persists in organizations and society disrupts the learning cycle at the heart of becoming a leader (Ibarra et al., 2013). Ibarra et al.'s (2013) research outlined steps that companies can take to rectify the situation. Yet, it is not enough to identify and instill the right skills and competencies as if in a social vacuum (Ibarra et al., 2013). The context must support a woman's motivation to lead and increase the likelihood that others will recognize and encourage her efforts even when she does not look or behave like senior executive's current generation (Ibarra et al., 2013). According to Ibarra et al., integrating leadership into one's core identity is particularly challenging for women, who must establish credibility in a deeply conflicted culture about whether, when, and how women should exercise authority. Ibarra et al. asserted the practices that equate leadership with behaviors considered more common in men indicate that women are not "cut out" to be leaders (p. 64). Furthermore, the human tendency to gravitate to people like oneself leads powerful men to sponsor and advocate for other men when leadership opportunities arise (Ibarra et al., 2013).

Carter-Sowell and Zimmerman (2015) suggested that despite a lack of discriminatory intent, subtle, second-generation forms of workplace gender bias can obstruct the leadership identity development of a company's entire population of women. The resulting underrepresentation of women in top positions reinforces entrenched beliefs, prompts and supports men's bids for leadership, and maintains the status quo (Carter-Sowell & Zimmerman, 2015). According to Ibarra et al. (2013), "More than 25 years ago, the social psychologist Faye Crosby stumbled on a surprising phenomenon: most women are unaware of having been victims of gender discrimination and deny it even when it is objectively true" (Ibarra et al., 2013, para. 1). Even the most enlightened women are unaware of having been victims of gender discrimination.

Rate of Change of Women in Leadership Positions

Women have worked hard to remove gender from the equation to recognize skills and talents (Carter-Sowell & Zimmerman, 2015). Moreover, gender bias in organizational policies and practices may suggest that women cannot determine personal success (Carter-Sowell & Zimmerman, 2015). In the upper tiers of organizations, women become increasingly scarce, heightening the visibility and scrutiny of those near the top, who may become risk-averse and overly focused on details and lose sense of purpose (Carter-Sowell & Zimmerman, 2015). Americans widely believe that men have a better chance at securing leadership positions in business and politics, even as majorities say that men and women make equally good leaders (Carter-Sowell & Zimmerman, 2015). However, according to Horowitz et al. (2018b), there is little consensus on why women remain underrepresented in these fields. About two-thirds of Americans, including the majority of men and women alike, state that it is easier for men to get elected to high political offices and to be awarded top executive positions in the business. Still, women are more likely to express this view (Horowitz et al., 2018a). About three-quarters of women say men have a better opportunity to secure these roles than about six in ten men surveyed, a pattern repeated across generations (Horowitz et al., 2018a).

Women are powerful agents of change (Devex, n.d.). The far-reaching benefits of diversity, gender parity in leadership, and decision-making are in all spheres. Still, women continue to be vastly under-represented in decision-making in politics, businesses, and communities (Devex, n.d.). According to Horowitz et al. (2018a), about six in 10 Americans believe there are too few women in high political offices at 59% and in top executive positions in business at 59% in the U.S. today. About one-third argue there is about the correct number of women in political leadership positions at 4% and 35% leadership positions (Horowitz et al.,

2018a). Small shares claim there are too many women in these roles, at 6% and 4%, respectively (Horowitz et al., 2018b). According to Devex (n.d.), women as leaders and decision-makers at all levels are critical to advancing gender justice and gender equality and to furthering economic, social, and political progress for all. When women are meaningfully represented and engaged in leadership bodies such as legislatures, courts, executive boards, the community council's laws, rulings, and decisions are more likely to be inclusive, representative, and take diverse views into account (Devex, n.d.).

One reason why more women are not moving into higher-up executive-type roles is the slack of female role model in the workplace (Wilson, 2019). Catalyst.org indicated that not having a visible role model can lead women to believe moving into a leadership-type role is simply unattainable (Wilson, 2019). Wilson (2019) argued race plays a significant role in considering and compensating in the workplace, as the pay a woman receives may vary depending on her race and ethnicity. Wilson shared that Asian/Pacific Islander women have the highest median annual earnings of $46,000. White women follow at $40,000, while Native American and Hispanic women have the lowest pay, earning $31,000 and $28,000 per year (Wilson, 2019). Earnings also vary by race as compared to how men are compensated (Wilson, 2019).

Gender inequity remains a challenge in the health workforce, with too few women making critical decisions and leading the work (Global Health Workforce Network, 2020). The Global Health Workforce Network and Women in Global Health today launched a report for the Commission on the Status of Women to describe the social and economic factors that may reflect why there are few women leaders in global health and to make an urgent call for action to address gender inequity (Global Health Workforce Network, 2020). According to the findings, women make up 70% of the health workforce, but only 25% hold senior roles (Global Health Workforce Network, 2020).

Gender and leadership behavior is a matter of great concern for organizations in recent years (Eagly et al., 1995). Eagly et al.'s (1995) research on gender differences in leadership behavior proved that women are more democratic or participative in leadership behavior, whereas men tend to adopt more autocratic or directive leadership styles. Eagly et al. stated that women are more concerned with maintaining interpersonal relationships and task accomplishment than men. A review of 86 studies about gender and leadership effectiveness indicated men and women do not differ in organizational effectiveness. Still, men were more effective in roles defined as masculine, and women were more effective in feminine roles (Eagly et al., 1995).

Likewise, organizational culture is another factor that can influence leadership behavior. One of the most important elements for developing strong corporate cultures is effective leadership (Kouzes & Posner, 2017). A leader, regardless of title, can be anybody who has influence or power, and leaders set the tone for corporate culture (Kouzes & Posner, 2017). Organizational culture and leadership have been theoretically and empirically interlinked (Martin, 2019). Many researchers have identified a constant interplay between corporate culture and leadership (Martin, 2019).

The U.S Department of Labor's Federal Glass Ceiling Commission, created in 1991 to address inequity in the workplace, identified that an "invisible barrier" was limiting women's access to career opportunities and advancement within organizations (Beckwith et al., 2016, p. 23). Research indicated that women hold from 1.3% to 5.1% of executive positions across the world (Berry & Franks, 2010). Within the U.S., 4% of women have CEO or senior leadership positions (Catalyst, 2007). A new study from McKinsey & Company and LeanIn.Org estimates that at the current rate, it may take about 25 years to reach gender parity in senior vice president roles and more than 100 years to do so in C-suite jobs (Devillard et al., 2019). In general, women have encountered sexism, discrimination, exclusion, and a lack of career advancement opportunities (Lyness & Grotto, 2018).

Stereotypes against women and discrimination can lead to significant problems in various dimensions of an organization, depending on its culture (Alvinius et al., 2017). Alvinius et al. (2017) identified potential barriers for women as leaders grouped into two main categories: work-family challenges and discrimination. White women may experience gender discrimination, whereas African American women may experience gender *and* racial discrimination (Beckwith et al., 2016). For African American women, the barriers of race and gender impact how African American women succeed in organizations. Beckwith et al. (2016) proffered White American women executives are driven to succeed and contribute to the many stereotypes and perceptions that hinder African American women executives. The stereotypes influence how African American women are promoted and, to some extent, the extent to which African American women are successful in those positions. However, recent research concluded that gender stereotypes have changed or are in the process of changing due to diversity training in organizations (Beckwith et al., 2016).

Consistent with social role theory (Eckes & Traunter, 2000) and social-cognitive research (Green, 2014), gender roles have pervasive effects. Not only is gender the personal characteristic that provides the most substantial basis for categorizing people, even when compared with race, age, and occupation, but also, stereotypes about women and men are quickly and automatically activated (Geiger & Kent, 2017). In recent years, the improvement of women's wages relative to men's likely reflects several broader changes in labor market dynamics with the stagnation of men's wages due to economic restructuring and industry globalization (Smith et al., 2019).

According to Stamarski & Son Hing (2015), potential causes consistent with the role congruity theory of prejudice included the lessening numerical tokenism of women in many management positions. The authors also recognized women's increasing power to make personnel decisions as owners of small businesses and decision-makers in larger organizations (Stamarski & Son Hing, 2015). In the year 2000, role congruity theory was proposed (Eagly & Karau, 2002). Eagly and Karau (2002) noted that groups are perceived positively when group members are congruent with characteristics aligned with typical social roles. Eagly and Karau extended the theory to include prejudice toward female leaders. The inconsistencies existing between the traits associated with female behavior were incongruous with factors related to organizational leadership. In modern society, men have traditionally occupied positions of power and influence (Eagly & Karau, 2002). Women, who now occupy nearly 50% of the workforce, hold lower-status positions (Powell & Butterfield, 2017). Pritlove et al. (2019) concluded that labor division gives rise to socially shared beliefs, gender roles, and congruous behavior in those roles. In the part congruity theory of prejudice, in leadership roles with relatively masculine definitions, women leaders are targets of two forms of discrimination: (a) a deficit in leadership ability and (b) the perception of women less favorably than men as potential occupants of leadership roles (Eagly & Karau, 2002).

A potential for prejudice exists when social perceivers hold a stereotype about a social group incongruent with the attributes deemed necessary for success in certain social roles classes (Eagly & Karau, 2002). When a stereotyped group member and an incongruent social part become joined in the perceiver's mind, this inconsistency lowers the group member's evaluation or potential occupant of the role (Eagly & Karau, 2002). In general, female leaders' prejudice follows from the contradiction that many people perceive between women's characteristics and the requirements of leadership roles. The feminine leadership style was called social-expressive, with personal attention paid to subordinates and focusing on the right work environment (Alvinius, 2017). In contrast, the masculine leadership style was described as an instrumental one, focused on giving directions (Alvinius, 2017).

Cascading gender bias theory identified leadership bias's potential to influence the organizational human resource management system (Reid et al., 2018). Warren (2009) described the double-bind dilemma and the unwritten rules to advancement as side effects of gender bias, preventing women from advancing to the executive suite. Warren identified three significant contributors to gender bias in talent management systems: (a) senior leadership effect, (b) institutionalizing bias, and (c) compounding bias. Schulz and Enslin (2014) noted:

Senior leadership effect describes two phenomena that contribute to cascading bias. First, because both male and female managers apply a thought leader–think male perspective to performance evaluation, women are disadvantaged when being considered for leadership positions, regardless of the gender of the hiring manager or influential organizational executive. Second, people generally prefer to work with and associate with others who share similar beliefs, values, and interests (Warren, 2009). Generally, people feel most comfortable with others most similar in lifestyle (p.16).

Consciously or subconsciously, organizational leaders apply gender stereotypes to establish preferences among potential candidates for executive openings and influence decisions about who is hired or promoted to top positions (Warren, 2009). Because most organizational executives are male, it stands to reason that the majority of individuals promoted to executive positions will also be male (Reid et al., 2018; Warren, 2009). Senior leadership effect influences who get assigned to high-visibility projects, participate in networking opportunities, and receive mentoring (Ibarra & Hunter, 2019; Warren, 2009).

The double-bind dilemma for women in leadership signifies that women in organizations struggle to overcome contradictory demands for performance, behavior, and direction (Catalyst, 2007). In *The Double-Bind Dilemma,* Catalyst (2007) described the phenomenon as:

> as a set of conflicting demands [requiring] women to demonstrate contradictory behaviors that set them up for harsh judgment no matter which action is adopted and forces them to choose between equally unsatisfactory alternatives. The double-bind manifests itself in three predicaments extreme perception, the high competence threshold, and competent but disliked and is manifest in masculine leadership theory and stereotypes. (p. 7)

Research focusing on conscious or deliberate biases toward women, particularly in workplace settings, has led to the study of unconscious bias (Ely et al., 2011). Unconscious gender bias, referred to as implicit or second-generation gender bias, occurs when a person consciously rejects gender "stereotypes but still unconsciously makes evaluations based on stereotypes" (American Association of University Women, 2016, p. 24). Today, many researchers believe that awareness of unconscious bias can help leaders fundamentally rethink how organizations approach strategic decision-making, organizational culture, inclusion, and talent management (Lew & Yousefi, 2017). Ely et al. (2011) found that women are less susceptible to unconscious bias's adverse effects once they become aware of how it manifests within an organization. (e.g., few role models, organization practices, suboptimal networks, and excessive performance pressure). And, in fact, most women are aware of these biases (Ely et al.,

2011). Program facilitators use standard leadership topics and tools (e.g., negotiations, leading change, networking, 360° feedback, and managing career transitions) to help women interpret acts through an unconscious bias lens to "facilitate women leaders' identity work and movement into leadership roles" (Ely et al., 2011, p. 475). Once women become conscious of their held biases, they can identify how biases are reinforced through structures, policies, and practices and can initiate change to impact organizations positively (Madsen & Andrade, 2018).

Gender stereotypes break down cognitive structures regarding how men and women process information (Kramer & Harris, n.d.). Further, men can be perceived as influencers to women advancing in leadership positions within the intercollegiate athletic administration (Rodriguez & Giuffrida, 2019). When one thinks of leadership characteristics and qualities a leader should possess, specific gender stereotypes are often directly related to leadership skills in their mind (Martin, 2019). Leaders can best be described through the lens of social role theory (Martin, 2019). Stereotypes about women and men are solely on gender (Kramer & Harris, n.d.). The stereotypes lead to the assignment of physical, mental, and emotional characteristics to gender. The traditional female stereotype is that women are communal, warm, pleasant, caregiving, gentle, modest, sensitive, and affectionate (Enwemeka, 2018). According to Alqahtani (2020), the traditional male stereotype is that men are agentic, strong, forceful, aggressive, competent, competitive, and independent. These conventional gender stereotypes operate in nearly all organizations in which women pursue careers (Kinyanjui, 2021). These stereotypes obstruct and block women's progress up the career ladder. Gender stereotypes in the workplace foster five distinct types of biases: (a) negative bias, (b) human bias, (c) agentic bias, (d) self-limiting bias, and (e) motherhood bias (Kramer & Harris, n.d.).

When supervisors, senior managers, and leaders in the C-suite of organizations hold negative stereotypes about women, they are likely to have low expectations about women's performance capability and potential (Saleem et al., 2017). These negative stereotypes limit or otherwise obstruct women's career advancement. Negative stereotypes obscure actual talents, ambition, and potential by ascribing the stereotypical communal characteristics while denying agentic characteristics (Lyness & Grotto, 2018). Because of this stereotypical reaction, women are often held to a higher standard than men in the workplace. Benevolent sexism arises from traditional gender stereotypes when gender stereotypes in the workplace are hidden by bias (Ibarra, 2021). When men perceive women as mild-mannered, gentle, and not incredibly competitive, they are likely to believe women need to be shielded from the aggressive demands characteristic of front-line business professionals' responsibility (Thorne, 2020).

On the contrary, when women behave with stereotypical male characteristics it often makes coworkers uncomfortable, causing them to think women are insensitive, abrasive, and disagreeable (Kallon, 2021). To avoid this stereotype, women tend to place self-limiting behaviors, resulting from stereotype threats (van Kralingen et al., 2021). This behavior causes women not to apply for upper-level positions fearing they are not qualified for the job (Ali, 2020). Ammerman and Groysberg (2021) stated that women too often choose work assignments and functions that involve less risk, lower visibility, fewer challenges, and less responsibility than those of male colleagues. Lastly, only 16% of Americans believe a mother should work full-time outside the home (Kramer & Harris, n.d.). Research by Kramer and Harris (n.d) noted in *The American Journal of Sociology* that mothers were significantly (79%) less likely to be hired and (100%) of those mothers were not promoted within organizations as well as being offered more than $10,000 less than women without families (Kramer & Harris, n.d.).

Thomas et al. (2020) discussed that despite gains for women in leadership, the *broken rung* was still a significant barrier in 2019 (p. 3). For the sixth year in a row in the United States, women continued to lose ground at the first step towards a management position. For every 100 men promoted to manager, only 85 women were encouraged (Thomas et al., 2020). This gap was even more significant for some women, as only 58 Black women and 71 Latinas were promoted (Thomas et al., 2020). As a result, women remained significantly outnumbered in entry-level management at the beginning of 2020, and women held just 38% of manager-level positions, while men held 62% (Thomas et al., 2020). Millions of women are considering downshifting careers or leaving the workforce. The broken rung, which has held millions of women back from being promoted to manager, is still broken. Black women are dealing with additional challenges—including long-standing racial bias issues—and getting less support from managers and co-workers (Thomas et al., 2020).

The leadership gap is universal though female representation varies by industry (Smith, 2021). According to Heilman (2012), women make up less than a quarter of STEM professionals. However, Heilman stated that women compose 62% of the workforce in health care but only hold 49% of leadership positions, which is a leadership gap of 13%. While the overall gender ratio can reveal barriers to entry, leadership gaps demonstrate obstacles to advancement.

Pew Research data indicate 15 female world leaders currently in office, eight of whom are country's first woman in power (Geiger & Kent, 2017). While the number of current female leaders, excluding monarchs and figurehead leaders, has more than doubled since 2000, these women still represent fewer than 10% of 193 UN member states (Geiger & Kent, 2017). The list of women currently in office includes nine heads of state and eight government heads (Geiger &

Kent, 2017). By 1991, the number of countries with some female leadership experience reached 20. Today, 70 countries have had some sort of female leadership (elected, appointed, interim, or other), including six of the world's 10 most populous countries (Geiger & Kent, 2017). The number of women running Fortune 500 companies has hit a record of 37. Geiger and Kent (2017) argue even though the number of females occupying CEO positions is up, only 7.4% of the Fortune 500 ranked businesses are compiled annually by the magazine. Geiger and Kent also proffered in 2018, 33 females occupied CEO positions, which was up from 24 positions the previous year. And 20 years ago, there were only two female-led companies (Geiger & Kent, 2017).

Biblical Integration

In the *New Living Translation* (NLT, 2019) version of Galatians 3:28, scripture records, "There is no longer Jew or Gentile, slave or free, male and female. For you are all one in Christ Jesus." There is neither the male nor the female that has any particular advantages for salvation. There are no favors shown on account of gender. This passage indicates that, particularly regarding salvation, men and women are equal.

According to Galatians (3:28) men and women stand as equals before God, both bearing the image of God Himself. However, God calls upon both men and women to fulfill the roles and responsibilities specifically designed for men and women without making one inferior to the other (NLT, 2019). Throughout the Bible, there are numerous women mentioned who demonstrated extraordinary leadership and courage.

- Deborah: A distinguished judge and leader of Israel.
- Huldah: A prophetess who changed a nation.
- Rahab: A discerning deliverer.

- Phoebe: A deacon of the church.

In fulfilling the divinely given roles taught in the New Testament, women are able to realize full potential because they are following the plan of God (NLT, 2019).

Chapter Summary

The number of women qualified for leadership roles is not translating into a higher representation of women in leadership roles (Diehl & Dzubinski, 2016). Research indicates that women are perceived as modestly more effective in education, government, and social services than in other organizations (Ramaswamy, 2020). Wilkie (2018) suggested that a career in which women may make the most leadership progress may be in higher education, where many women make inroads into leadership positions. Some researchers seek to examine which leadership styles are better for women by re-defining leadership styles typically associated with feminine characteristics. Kray et al. (2017) called for a gender-holistic leadership model. Kray et al. proposed that women are better suited to the features and traits assigned to servant or resonant leadership style roles than the more directive or transactional functions. Kray et al. sought to reduce gender equality by introducing the servant leadership style into organizational leadership as a gender-neutral leadership style.

In the business, political, military, and other social spheres, leadership has traditionally been a male privilege (Eagly & Karau, 2002). Although women have gained increased access to supervisory and middle management positions, they remain relatively rare as elite leaders and top executives (Kennedy, 2018). A cultural and science debate has raised the possibility of a "glass ceiling," a potential pillar of sexism that blocks women from advanced leadership roles (Eagly, 1987, p.756). The popularity of the glass ceiling concept may stem from women's rarity in significant leadership posts, despite the presence of equality or near equality of gender on many other indicators (U.S. Department of Labor, 1995). Several statistics indicate that there is gender equality in the United States, as women make up 46% of all workers (Mastracci, 2017).

Explanations for the sparse representation of women in elite leadership roles traditionally focused on the idea that a lack of qualified women created a "pipeline problem" (Eagly & Karau, 2002, p. 1). This shortage of women is ascribed to various causes, including women's family responsibilities (Devillard et al., 2019). Olsson and Martiny (2018) stated that a barrier exists in women's inherited tendencies to display fewer traits and motivations to attain and achieve success in high-level positions. Women's roles in society changed significantly in the 1970s and 1980s (Lew & Yousefi, 2017). More than half of all women work outside the home, and traditionally male professions have been infused with a small portion of women (Fetters et al., 1984). In recent years, it has become clear that organizations must tap women's resources and abilities to accommodate the changing workplace of the 1990s (Lew & Yousefi, 2017).

The purpose of this literature review was to inform the reader about the factors that may contribute to women's underrepresentation in leadership roles. By drawing from definitions commonly used in the relevant research, this qualitative phenomenological research study defined language within the dissertation and maintained the intended context. After a careful examination of relevant literature gathered through scholarly study, the study's questions remain.

Research findings indicated that equality is currently less available to women under male-dominated hierarchies due to a lack of findings to address the issues. Women have been disregarded in terms of professional growth and conscious grooming in preparation for advancement. The literature lacked findings on the outcome of the lived experience of women who progressed to leadership positions and how barriers and biases impacted their personal trajectory and factors that contributed to sustainability in the position. Finding an answer to

"What are the factors that may contribute to women's underrepresentation in leadership roles?" remains an area in need of further research.

In Chapter 3, the study describes the qualitative phenomenology methodology selected for this research process and provides an explanation for the choice of the data sample, along with a definition of the analysis unit. The chapter features the rationale regarding the instrument used to collect the data and information on its validity and reliability. The techniques for gathering and analyzing the data are also discussed.

CHAPTER 3: RESEARCH METHODOLOGY

Despite decades of progress relative to men in the workplace and the political arena, women remain severely underrepresented among top corporate and political leaders (Averett et al., 2017). This doctoral study examined the current status and recent progress of women in leadership positions, focusing on corporate leadership. The purpose of this chapter is to provide an overview of the research methodology used to explore the lived experiences of women overlooked for leadership positions in workplaces.

Statement of the Problem

The problem is that the barriers and biases contributing to the scarcity of senior female leadership in private industry and governmental organizations across the United States are not known. This study aimed to address the barriers and biases that exist in the female leadership gap, particularly in government and private businesses. "Achieving gender parity in leadership is, first and maybe most importantly, an issue of fairness," according to the AAUW (2020, p. 2). Leaders are determining how the dynamics of our society will evolve in the future. Suppose women are not recognized for their abilities, regardless of gender. In that case, the opportunity to use those abilities is denied, which negatively influences our society on a worldwide scale (AAUW, 2020). Women have made significant progress toward reaching gender equality in the workplace, and they now account for over 46% of the workforce (Bureau of Labor Statistics, 2015). "Men are significantly more likely than women to climb to the highest paying and most prominent leadership jobs in practically any industry," according to AAUW (2020, p. 19). Across the country, there is a leadership diversity disparity between men and women in senior positions (Warner et al., 2018). The fact that women are known to perform better than men, in general, does not appear to impact women's ability to lead, according to Warner et al. (2018).

Since 1988, women have outnumbered men on college campuses, have obtained at least one-third of law degrees since 1980, and have made up one-third of medical school students by 1990 (Warner et al., 2018). (Warner et al., 2018).

Women executives contribute to a company's bottom line rather than detract from it (Dezsö & Ross, 2012). Dezsö and Ross (2012) evaluated management data from S&P 1500 enterprises with and without at least one woman in top management over 15 years. With only one woman in senior leadership, the firm's performance improved (Dezsö & Ross, 2012). Women are more likely to have unique abilities, such as risk management and failure tolerance, and unique attributes, such as creativity, intelligence, and emotional stability (Watson & Detjen, 2021). Combined with women's more significant education and professional credentials, these talents show that women are suitable candidates for leadership positions (Saleem et al., 2017). Despite this, women in America have not attained the prominence or positions of power that they should have due to their educational achievements (Warner et al., 2018).

In many industries, women's representation in top leadership positions such as law partners, medical school deans, and business executive officers maintains between 5% and 20%. (Warner et al., 2018). Overall, there is a vast disparity between the fortunes of a small number of notable women at the top of their sectors and the fortunes of most women across the country (Warner et al., 2018). The gap between American women and male counterparts in peer countries is widening (Warner et al., 2018). Although women receive more college degrees than males, they are underrepresented in positions of power and leadership (Warner et al., 2018). The imbalance in gender representation in senior leadership in governmental organizations and commercial enterprises across the United States is the subject of this study, as are the reasons contributing to this paucity.

Research Method and Design

When seeking to better understand the human condition, with all the problems this enterprise poses for traditional scientific research approaches, qualitative research is considered superior to the more rigorous quantitative research (Caelli, 2001). Investigators who use phenomenological approaches to understand human healing experiences, caring, and wholeness need to consider the differences between descriptive and hermeneutic phenomenology (Creswell & Creswell, 2018). Using a phenomenological research design, this study explored and described the lived experiences of 13 women who were overlooked for leadership positions in the workplace. Although women outperform men in the number of educational degrees earned, women are not at the same level in power and leadership hierarchy (Advantages & Disadvantages, 2020).

The central phenomena explored in this study are factors that lead to the underrepresentation of women in leadership positions who are as equally qualified as male counterparts. The study focused on understanding how participants approach an issue or problem in a specific context or setting. Creswell and Creswell (2018) recommended using a qualitative method for this type of research. Unlike the quantitative method, which focuses on causation, the qualitative design focuses on explanation (Creswell & Creswell, 2018). Qualitative research gives voice to the research participants, allowing participants to share experiences (Creswell & Creswell, 2018). Open-ended research questions were designed specifically to reveal the experiences and perceptions of women who face the challenges of competing with men in the workplace. A qualitative research design consists of several approaches. Creswell and Creswell identified a few common methods, including ethnography, grounded theory, and phenomenology.

Research Design

Even though a quantitative research design was considered for this study, it was not selected. There are disadvantages to applying a quantitative research approach to a study (Creswell & Poth, 2018). The quantitative approach is used when researchers seek answers to specific questions to prove or disprove a particular hypothesis (Lune & Berg, 2018). Still, quantitative research does not focus on people's motives when sharing an opinion or making decisions (Creswell & Clark, 2018).

The mixed approaches technique has flaws as well (Dodgson, 2019). The mixed way of analysis is more expensive and time-consuming than any other research method, according to Pros and Cons (2017). According to Pros and Cons (2017):

> Firstly, owning to its duplicity content, applying the mixed methodology in one study can prove challenging to handle by any single researcher. This is the case, especially when the researcher has two use two or more approaches concurrently. Furthermore, a researcher who chooses to rely on this research method has to learn about multiple methods and techniques and understand how to mix them appropriately. (para. 27)

Case studies, grounded theory, and ethnography are examples of qualitative research designs that might be acceptable for this subject, will not be used. Several objections were leveled towards single case study analysis, the most prominent of which center on the intertwined issues of methodological rigor, researcher subjectivity, and external validity (Creswell & Creswell, 2018).

The grounded theory approach explains a process or phenomenon based on the participant's perspective (Creswell, 2009). According to Creswell and Creswell (2018), the grounded theory strategy is the best strategy to use when no theory explains the study's issue.

The grounded theory was not used as this research study's focus was not to generate a theory but rather to explore experiences.

The ethnographic approach focuses on describing and interpreting beliefs, values, and behaviors of a culture-shaping group within the context of culture (Creswell & Creswell, 2018). Ethnography requires studying a culture-sharing group over a prolonged period within a natural setting (Moustakas, 1994). Ethnography was not selected, as it was unlikely that the participants shared the same cultural experiences. The ethnographic approach would not provide the data needed to answer the research questions.

The approach of this phenomenological qualitative research study allowed for a deeper understanding of the imbalance of gender representation in leadership positions for women effected by education, job performance, politics, salary, and family dynamics. The applicability of phenomenology for this study is further discussed in this chapter. The research plan, which includes the methodology, participants, procedures, and analysis method, is also a component of this chapter. The following research questions explored women's challenges with stereotypical views of female behavior as they aspire to executive leadership roles in private and public sectors. To discover the extent to which parallels in women's experiences with bias or prejudice exist, the answers may lead to a possible reason for the underrepresentation of women's leadership. This was a crucial moment of discovery for women aspiring to executive leadership in the corporate and public sectors.

- RQ1: How do women mentorship programs influence women in attaining top leadership positions in private and political sectors?
- RQ2: What support do women need to attain successful careers as leaders?

- RQ3: How does the representation of women in higher levels of leadership impact the views and beliefs on women's leadership roles?
- RQ4: What are the various factors motivating or limiting women in attaining top leadership positions in private and public sectors?
- RQ5: How does a woman's family dynamics affect her leadership role compared to her male counterparts?

The researcher exploring the lived experiences of 13 women who were overlooked for leadership positions in the workplace and utilized the research questions in Table 1 (Appendix A) to answer the research questions. The open-ended research questions were designed specifically to reveal the experiences and perceptions of women who faced challenges competing with men in the workplace.

According to Adu (2019), phenomenology must be an in-depth, thorough process to capture and describe the whole meaning and understanding of an individual's experiences. Adu articulated how the phenomenological strategy can capture persons' emotions and perspectives about a particular phenomenon that others experience (Bloomberg & Volpe, 2019). Data are most often collected through in-depth interviews with multiple individuals (Bloomberg & Vople, 2019). Creswell (2013) recommended interviewing between 5–25 individuals who have shared a particular phenomenon. Creswell and Creswell (2018) also noted that knowing the experiences of healthcare personnel, policymakers, and family women is beneficial. This insight will identify and inform policy practices, which was the focus of this study.

Participants

The problem this study sought to address were barriers and biases that lead to the female leadership gap, specifically in governmental organizations and private industries. The purposeful sampling strategy was applied to examine the lived experiences of women impacted by the circumstances facing barriers and biases in achieving senior leadership positions. According to Bloomberg and Volpe (2019), in criterion sampling, "participants are chosen because they meet a certain set of criteria as predetermined by the researcher" (p. 385). To be considered for this study, several criteria factors had to be met. The potential participants had to be a female between the ages of 30–65. The participants needed to be representative of various ethnic, socioeconomic, and religious backgrounds. The female participants had to be working professionals with a minimum of a college-level degree in business, political science, engineering, math, or a related subject who continued their careers in a related profession. The participants must have worked in their related profession for a minimum of 3 years.

According to Adu (2019), unlike the simple random sample and the systematic random sample, some researchers "are interested in particular strata (meaning groups) within the population (e.g., males vs. females, houses vs. apartments, etc.)" (as cited in dan Kluster, 2015, para. 1). Purposeful sampling is widely used in qualitative research for the identification and selection of information-rich cases related to the phenomenon of interest (Bloomberg & Volpe, 2019). Each stratum is then sampled using another probability sampling method, such as cluster or simple random sampling, allowing the study to estimate statistical measures for each sub-population. The strata was divided based on members' shared attributes or characteristics, such as leadership positions in the workplace.

Using social media platforms, the study invited women who met the designed criterion sampling to participate in interviews concerning their experiences as women in leadership in governmental organizations and private industries. As the platform for recruitment allowed a national reach, randomizing the sample prevented unfairly selecting one particular demographic, which may have different qualities or opinions than the general population. By drawing a random sample from a larger population, the goal was that the sample was representative of the larger group and less likely to be subject to bias.

The sample was composed of women between the ages of 30 and 65 from various ethnic, socioeconomic, and religious backgrounds. The number of years participants had been in a leadership position was not a variable. Female professionals with a college-level degree in business, political science, engineering, math, or a related subject, who continued careers in a related profession, were the target population to participate.

The relevant stratification for this study was job promotion between men and women in the workplace. The study examined the opportunities afforded to women seeking leadership positions. To complete the study, a participant letter (Appendix C) was issued to women who responded with interest to participate in the study accompanied by the Consent Form (Appendix D). After the executed consent form was returned by the participant, the questionnaire was electronically distributed to prospective participants to participate in the study (Appendix B).

As with the simple random sampling and systematic random sampling techniques, a consecutive number from 1 to N was assigned for each participant. There was a sample size of 13 women. The sample is expressed as n. This number was chosen because of the time limit to distribute the questionnaire to the women and receive authentic feedback.

Instruments

According to Bloomberg and Volpe (2019), multiple data-gathering strategies are typically utilized in qualitative research as a purposeful strategy to generate a more sophisticated knowledge of the phenomenon under investigation. Triangulation strengthens a study by combining methods (Moustakas, 1994). The triangulation method is a critical strategy for improving the quality of data from multiple sources, in various ways, with the hope that the practice will provide an in-depth understanding of the phenomenon under study by illuminating different facets of situations and experiences. Triangulation also assists in portraying said experiences and circumstances authentically, in their entirety, and in complexity (Bloomberg & Volpe, 2019). To ensure triangulation of this phenomenological qualitative study, there were three methods employed: questionnaires, semi-structured interviews, and observational field notes.

According to Groenewald (2004), phenomenology starts with a synopsis of the research paradigm. Following the data-gathering methods is a definition of where to locate test subjects, accompanied by data-storage methods. Next follows an explanation of the explication of the data (comprising several stages). Interviews, conversations, subject observation, behavior studies, focus meetings, and personal text analysis are some of the tools that can be used in phenomenologically focused research (Groenewald, 2004). In this study, the focus of the interviews was to is to seize and articulate women's narratives/stories fully.

In preparation for the interview process, a pilot study was conducted. A pilot study is one of the essential stages in a research project (Hassan et al., 2006). A pilot study, in a research project, is conducted to identify potential problem areas and deficiencies in the research instruments and protocol prior to implementation during the full study (Hassan et al., 2006). The pilot study focused on ensuring there was no ambiguity in the interview questions and that participants will feel comfortable answering the questions phrased in the manner constructed.

The study was comprised of a 10-item questionnaire that was distributed to each selected participant. The interviews consist of open-ended questions to explore women's work experiences and the desire to obtain leadership positions (Appendix A). Responses to the interview questions posed answered the respective research questions (Table 1).

Table 1

Research Questions and Interview Question Chart

RESEARCH QUESTIONS	CORRELATING INTERVIEW QUESTION(S)
Q1. How do female mentorship programs influence women in attaining top leadership positions in private and public sectors?	Interview Questions 1 & 3
Q2. What support do women need to attain successful careers as leaders?	Interview Question 9
Q3: How does the representation of women in higher levels of leadership impact the views and beliefs on women's leadership roles?	Interview Questions 6, 7, & 8
Q4: What are the various factors motivating or limiting women in attaining top leadership positions in private and public sectors?	Interview Questions 2 & 4
Q5. How does a woman's family dynamics affect her leadership role compared to her male counterparts?	Interview Question 5

Note. The above questions show the correlation between the research questions and interview questions.

The first section focused on each respondent's current status, including years of experience, degrees obtained, definitions of leadership, leadership styles, and how these definitions have influenced workplace behavior. The questions allowed for an exploration of any incongruence between domestic roles and leadership roles. The designed questions enabled participants to describe experiences with bias about stereotypical female behavior to obtain career goals.

The second section of the questionnaire focused on career promotion opportunities. A forced ranking scale method is the preferred method for respondents to decide on several possibilities (Lau & Kennedy, 2021). The responses were recorded as (1) *rarely*, (2) *seldom*, (3) *sometimes*, (4) *frequently*, or (5) *very frequently*. The responses helped generalize leadership opportunities that may be more common with specific individuals.

Table 2

Qualitative Plan

Research Questions	Independent Factors	Dependent Factors	Data Source
Q1: How do female mentorship programs influence women in attaining top leadership positions in private and public sectors?	Female Business Leader	Leadership Role	Job Titles
Q2: What support do women need to attain successful careers as leaders?	Female Business Leader	Leadership Role	Job Titles
Q3: How does the representation of women in higher levels of leadership impact the views and beliefs on women's leadership roles?	Female Business Leader	Leadership Role	Job Titles
Q4: What are the various factors motivating or limiting women in attaining top leadership positions in private and public sectors?	Female Business Leader	Leadership Role	Job Titles
Q5: How does a woman's family dynamics affect her leadership role compared to her male counterparts?	Female Business Leader	Leadership Role	Job Titles

Note. The above questions list points of inquiry posed by this doctoral study. It identifies the participants of the study and lists the category regarding the participants' roles.

There was a brief description of the study participants' domestic roles and leadership roles. Participants completed a qualitative questionnaire as well as an interview. The electronic questionnaire process took no longer than 15 minutes. The interview, which was conducted through a virtual meeting setting, lasted approximately one hour. The meeting was recorded via Zoom, a video conferencing platform, with written permission from the participant. The questionnaire results were pooled for the dissertation research, and the individual results of this study remain confidential and anonymous. Should this study be published, only pooled results will be documented. There were no costs incurred by either the individual participants or their respective organization.

With written consent from each participant, all information collected from interviews was recorded. The recorded interviews were transcribed by the transcription service NVivo 12, a professional transcription service that provided the study's data in a PDF after completing the transcription. Detailed observational field notes were kept from the interviews to indicate each participant's perceptions and feelings. The transcribed interview was sent to the research participants for approval to ensure an accurate reflection of the study participants' thoughts and wording.

According to Princeton Research, Research Integrity and Assurance (2020), when people or organizations exchange data files, there is a higher risk of exposed confidential data. The most challenging part of any data backup plan is transferring or copying the data to new sites. The way data is shared and processed should be considered when determining how sensitive a method

(Princeton Research, Research Integrity and Assurance, 2020). While moving confidential research files to another location, the most crucial thing to remember is constantly compressing and encrypting the data to reduce unauthorized entry risk (Princeton Research, Research Integrity and Assurance, 2020). The study maintained the participants' corresponding file names for accompanying the content when transferring files as attachments to or saving files on physical media such as CDs or flash drives. Since it limited the file downloads' scale, this was also useful in minimizing the risk of the file upload failing. Since the file is encrypted with a password and only someone with authorization may access the extended edition, someone not been permitted to read it cannot access the data. The use of SharePoint or sponsored Google Drive was another reliable and easy file transfer method.

After any research project, varying regulations dictate the length of time records should be kept. It is essential to archive reports for the longest time indicated in the federal statute. Some federal laws require documents to be achieved for three years, while others require archival for no less than five years (U. S. Department of Justice Archives, 2020). Columbia International University requires records be archived for three years. Research data will be destroyed in a manner that leaves no possibility for reconstruction of information. Appropriate methods for destroying/disposing of paper records include: burning, shredding then cross shredding, pulping, and pulverizing. The appropriate methodology for destroying digital data is through deleting or overwriting information, purging magnetic media through degaussing (exposure to a strong magnetic field), or destroying the physical media.

Research Procedures

As cited in *Phenomenological Research Methods*, Moustakas's (1994) modification of van Kaam's 1987 psychophenomenological model (PPM) for analyzing phenomenological data was used for this study. The process for analyzing phenomenological data consisted of the following steps using each participant's transcript:

1. There should be a listing of responses (expressions) that was relevant to the participant's experience.
2. There should be an individual structural description of each participant's experience based on the individual responses.
3. The should be structural descriptions developed comprised of a composite description of the experiences reflective of the entire participant population.

Selection criteria for each individual required that: (1) the participant identified as a female, (2) the participant was currently employed or had been employed in a top-level leadership position within the past 10 years, and (3) the participant was between the ages of 30–65. The sampling procedure was, therefore, a criterion-based or purposive sampling.

The individuals were invited to participate via a study's posting on LinkedIn and Facebook pages. Personal emails with a request to participate were sent to the respondents from the social media postings. After the participants agreed to join the study, a second contact was made by email to disseminate the consent form. Upon receipt of the executed consent form, the questionnaire was distributed along with a calendar for potential participants to select a date and time to meet for the individual interview. At the time of the second contact, a discussion of the purpose of the research occurred to ensure that the participants had a clear understanding of the study's purpose to make an informed consent to participate. A signed informed consent form was obtained.

In qualitative research, using the constructivist worldview allows each participant to share the participant's story as experienced, instead of fitting personal experience into a single-correct-answer perspective (Power & Gendren, 2015). Once adapted for this study, an expert in gender studies conducted member-checking of the interview questions to ensure alignment with the research questions. This review lead to slight adjustments to the research questions to ensure coalition.

Once the observational field notes and interviews were completed, the recorded interviews were transcribed with the transcription services of NVivo 12. Files of the transcriptions were sent to participants for review. If participants found that any areas of the transcriptions were not representative of expressed thoughts, the transcription were reviewed and modified to accurately depict the expression of the participant. Upon review, participants responded with written approval of the accuracy of statements.

The focus was to cross-examine these transcriptions qualitatively, seeking the participants' experiences, opinions, attitudes, beliefs, and perceptions regarding the factors affecting the inability to be promoted to higher leadership positions within companies. This section concludes with a phenomenological description that correlates women's underrepresentation in leadership roles to the description, understanding, and interpretation of the meaning of participants' life experiences.

Data Analysis Strategy

Permission to disseminate the questionnaire was obtained by formulating the appropriate permission documentation, completing the required information about the study, and asking the appropriate person to contact the membership. There was also a request to document the approval. It took approximately one month to complete this task. Questionnaires were emailed to the participants. Each questionnaire was emailed with a cover letter that concisely outlined the research's purpose, how the data would be used, and plans for maintaining the respondents' confidentiality. Participants were given 10 days to complete and return the questionnaires. Courtesy emails were sent to follow up with participants who had not completed the questionnaire within the 10-day window. This study's response rate was 85–90%, which was also needed to complete the study efficiently.

When conducting qualitative research, transcribing interviews and other audio files is essential but can be highly time-consuming. To accomplish this critical component, NVivo 12 was employed. NVivo 12 Transcription's intuitive editor was used to allow for changes, tagging speakers, and ensuring that the transcription was formatted correctly.

To preserve the data analysis's quality and trustworthiness, participants were given a copy of the transcript to review and check for errors and confirm the accuracy of the information provided. The participants also had the opportunity to provide feedback on the individual descriptions to ensure accurate delivery of what the participant was trying to express through the interview. The study did not interpret the data in a biased nature.

For this study, the responsiveness established credibility. The study needed to use sensitivity, creativity, and insight, be open-minded and be willing to relinquish ideas that are not supported, regardless of personal opinions (Morse et al., 2002). To verify that the sample studied was adequate, this study consisted of participants who best represented the knowledge sought for this research. All the women chosen for this study had credentials equal to a male coworker, leading to leadership positions within companies. Having these foundational credentials similar to male-counterparts ensures "efficient and effective saturation of categories, with optimal quality data and minimum dross" (Morse et al., 2002, p. 12).

Delimitations

According to Creswell and Poth (2018) delimitations focus the scope or boundaries of a researcher's study. The research design was expressly limited to the population of women in higher leadership levels of the corporate and political spectrums. This was a purposive sampling, interviewing only those who volunteered and who held senior-level leadership. For this study, there were three delimitations for participants. Participants must be: female in gender, be between the age of 30–65, and have experience holding a leadership position, which is identified as director-level or higher. Moreover, only those participants who were willing to participate in the study were selected. This measured prevented participants from declining in the middle of the study, resulting in unfinished and unusable data.

Ethical Issues

Based on the Belmont Report Protections (Office for Human Research Protections, 2016), the ethical principles of respect for persons, beneficence, and justice was honored throughout the research study. Before any contact with participants, an Institutional Review Board (IRB) approval (Office for Human Research Protections, 2016) was obtained. Written informed consent forms were sent to participants. Before the interview, after the participant's written consent was received, an email and a telephone conversation was conducted to explain the study's purpose more thoroughly and schedule a time and place for the interview. During the telephone conversations, additional time was provided to allow participants to ask further questions. This protocol enabled participants to make an informed decision regarding participation in the study and confirm clear understanding of the study's purpose, possible risks, and confidentiality terms. There was no physical risk to the participants during the interview as the interview was conducted in the participant's chosen environment. To minimize the possible emotional risk of sensitivity to an interview question asked, the participants were informed of their right to stop the interview at any time (Office for Human Research Protections, 2016).

Chapter Summary

This phenomenological study explored the challenges women face when overlooked for leadership positions. The study may provide essential and applicable insight for women who seek promotions to leadership positions by exploring the various avenues and options of moving to the top of a professions. Hattery (2001) stated that women hold a prominent place in the workforce, while the highest offices in the nation are still being filled primarily by men; yet, the possibility and promise of women in leadership is rising. According to Hattery, "Women can be successful professionally as well as in their roles as mothers when supported by partners, family, friends, child care teammates, and those in their workplace in their efforts to weave work and family" (p. 187). Chapter 4 describes the analysis process and the study's results.

CHAPTER 4: ANALYSIS & RESULTS

The purpose of this qualitative phenomenology study was to explore the barriers and biases faced by women while attaining leadership positions in governmental organizations and private industries. The problem this study sought to address was the barriers and biases of the female leadership gap specifically in governmental organizations and private industries. Gaining new knowledge about women's lived experiences with gender bias and role stereotyping may benefit future generations of women aspiring to senior levels of organizational leadership. Obtaining information about participants' career progression was accomplished by asking semi-structured questions about the participant's leadership journey:

- RQ1: How do women mentorship programs influence women in attaining top leadership positions in private and political sectors?
- RQ2: What support do women need to attain successful careers as leaders?
- RQ3: How does the representation of women in higher levels of leadership impact the views and beliefs on women's leadership roles?
- RQ4: What are the various factors motivating or limiting women in attaining top leadership positions in private and public sectors?
- RQ5: How does a woman's family dynamics affect her leadership role compared to her male counterparts?

In this chapter, the research provided the opportunity to presents the results of the completed analysis and data collected from participants of the study. This chapter begins with an introduction to the study which describes the participant sample and anonymity. The display of data progresses to the research methodology applied for data analysis and a discussion of how it was conducted. The information gathered is presented in terms of emergent themes that offer a sense of the totality. The chapter ends with a summary of the findings and a segue to Chapter 5's discussion of the discoveries' broader implications.

The methodology of the study was qualitative and phenomenological. Thirteen female leaders in executive positions from across the United States participated in an individual interview process resulting in rich data for the study. The qualitative phenomenological method also allowed for the exploration of leaders' educational background, industry experience, position seniority, and experiences regarding career barriers.

There is no scarcity of qualified female leaders. Women account for over half of the labor force in the United States (Martineau & Mount, 2019). Women outnumber males in bachelor's and master's degrees and are almost equal in the number of earned medical and law degrees. Yet, from corporate boardrooms to Congress, health-care firms to the courts, non-profit organizations to colleges, men are considerably more likely than women to advance to the highest-paid and most prominent leadership positions. Through this research, the opportunity to gain new knowledge and perspectives about women's experiences with gender biases and role stereotyping may significantly benefit current and future generations of women aspiring to roles in organizational leadership.

This chapter includes discussions concerning the analysis conducted and its consistency with the qualitative phenomenology research design and its connection to the research questions. This chapter describes the process used to analyze transcripts from the 13 individual interviews, which led to the identified codes and themes. The chapter also includes an introduction to the qualitative descriptive research study regarding factors that may cause the underrepresentation of women in leadership positions. Also included in this chapter is background information that highlights the underrepresentation of women in leadership roles and supports the rationale for conducting the research. The problem and purpose statements outline the issues associated with a disproportionate number of women achieving leadership positions for which women are qualified compared to their male counterparts. Discussion includes the strategy to interview successful women and determine the appropriate sample size to complete the study. The study analyzed the ideas, feelings, and individual experiences participants experienced when denied the opportunity to obtain a leadership position.

In Chapter 4, the study offered a more detailed explanation of the research methodology regarding the data collection process. The study's purpose in conducting this research study was to explore the effect of factors that hinder women from advancing socially, economically, politically, and professionally. The purpose of Chapter 4 was to also provide a restatement of the purpose and research questions, followed by the results of the research question, and a summary.

Descriptive Data

The study investigated data from 13 participants from around the United States. The participants were selected through purposive sampling of women who identified themselves as leaders based on current or previous job experiences and positions. According to Creswell and Clark (2018), transcripts of interviews sometimes run into the hundreds of pages, as do extensive observational field notes. All data needed rigorous scrutiny, detailed interpretation, and complex synthesis. Qualitative analysis elicits the discovery of patterns, consistent themes, meaningful categories, and novel concepts (Creswell & Clark, 2018). Sound analysis elicits a comprehensive knowledge of a phenomenon or process (Creswell & Clark, 2018). The study of detailed descriptions throughout a project frequently reveals fresh views, and its examination of interconnected themes may yield helpful insights.

This research study considered 13 female participants from around the United States who self-identified as leaders based on current or previous job positions and experiences. To learn more about the distribution of the sample considered for the study, demographic information was collected for purposive sampling and ease into the semi-structured interview session. Table 3 illustrates the demographic data of the participants:

Table 3

Demographic Data

Participant	Education	YOB	Age	Pursuing Higher Ed.	Professional Experience	Sector	Participation in Mentorship Programs	Affiliation Female Leader
Participant 1	Doctorate	1974	47	No	25	Private	Yes	No
Participant 2	Master's	1973	48	Yes	20	Private	Yes	No
Participant 3	Master's	1972	49	No	24	Public	No	Yes
Participant 4	Bachelor's	1956	65	No	36	Private	No	No
Participant 5	Master's	1975	46	No	20	Public	Yes	Yes
Participant 6	Doctorate	1977	44	No	17	Private	Yes	No
Participant 7	Master's	1981	40	No	15	Public	No	Yes
Participant 8	Doctorate	1971	50	No	16	Public	No	No
Participant 9	Bachelor's	1973	48	No	17	Private	Yes	Yes
Participant 10	Doctorate	1962	59	No	26	Private	Yes	Yes
Participant 11	Bachelor's	1969	52	No	30	Private	Yes	Yes
Participant 12	Doctorate	1970	51	No	20	Public	Yes	Yes
Participant 13	Doctorate	1968	53	No	15	Private	Yes	No

Participants were identified in age ranges from 40–65, as detailed below. Relevant descriptions are included in Table 4.

Table 4

Age of the Participants

Age		
40–44	2	15%
45–49	5	38%
50–54	4	31%
55–59	1	8%
60–64	0	0%
65 >	1	8%
Total	13	100%

The study participants' ages ranged between 40 and 65 years. The age group between 45 and 49 had the highest number of participants with 38% (5) of the participants, while those above 60 years represented 8% (1).

Figure 1

Age of Participants

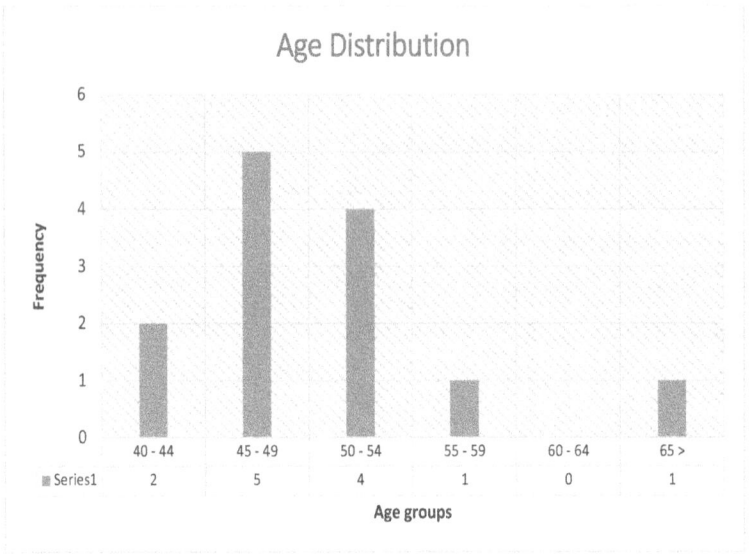

Education Status of the Participants

After assessing the education status of the participants for this research study, it was noted that the majority of the participants, at 46% (6), had achieved a doctorate level. In comparison, only 23% (3) had a bachelor's degree as the highest level of education. Figure 2 summarizes the education status among the sample considered.

Figure 2

Education Level of Participants

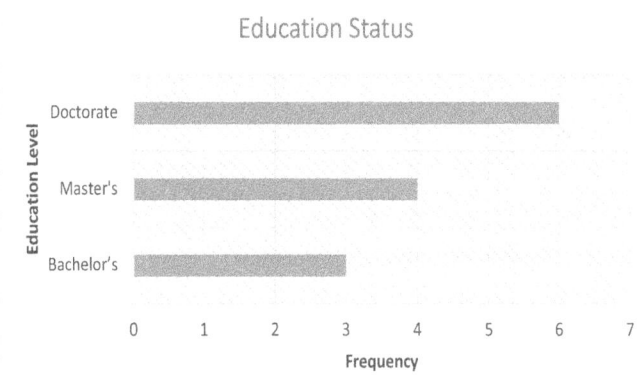

Pursuing Higher Education

Only one participant was pursuing higher education, indicating that several participants were not interested in advancing education. Figure 3 summarizes participants who are seeking higher levels of education:

Figure 3

Participants Pursuing Higher Education

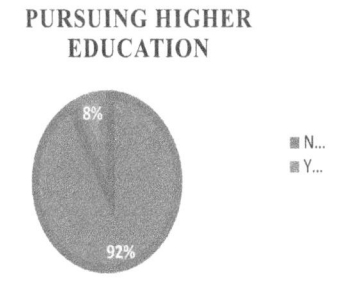

Participation in Mentorship Programs

Women are critical candidates for filling the leadership pipeline and C-suite benches that will soon be left empty by a leaving generation of employees, accounting for 47% of the existing workforce and rising (Chronus, 2021). Women must acquire many critical abilities to overcome certain prejudices and difficulties in order to flourish inside careers and during the mid-career marathon. Mentoring can provide a forum for discussing how to confront these issues with confidence (Chronus, 2021).

Figure 4

Participation in Mentorship Programs

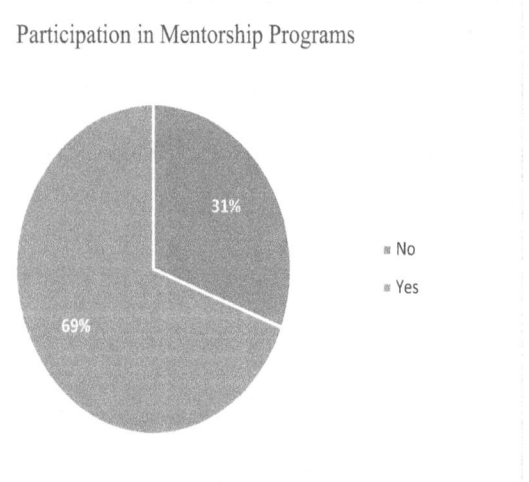

Figure 4 above summarizes the findings that indicate 69% (9) of the participants had participated in mentorship programs, as shown in the graph.

Figure 5

Participants' Sector of Operation

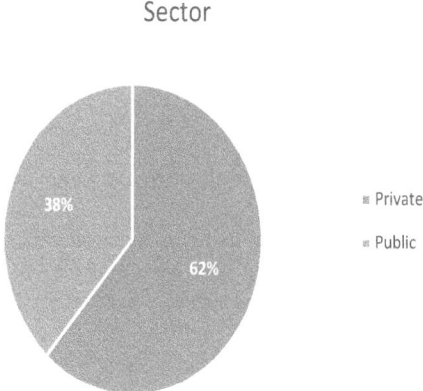

From Figure 5 above, it can be noted that the most participants at 62% came from the private sector.

Figure 6 summarizes the affiliation the participants held with female leadership organizations.

Figure 6

Affiliation with Female Leadership Organizations

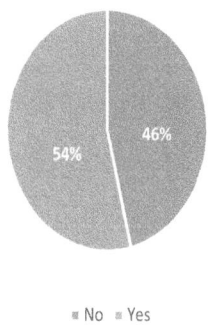

The graphical representation in Figure 6 indicates that 54% (7) of the participants had an affiliation with female leadership organizations.

Data Analysis Procedures

Using a qualitative study approach, the study participants' attitudes, beliefs, and opinions were investigated. Lived experiences were explored using individual, semi-structured interviews. By conducting the qualitative interview based on these attributes, the study depicted the knowledge structures based on reflective analysis and interpretation of the research participants' accounts. Data obtained from each interview were then analyzed to elicit a deeper understanding of the meaning related to the participants' lived experiences. The qualitative data analysis involved the general themes observed from participants' attitudes, beliefs, and opinions. The NVivo 12 software was effective in the qualitative data analysis process by transcribing, coding, analyzing, and interpreting the data collected from the semi-structured interviews. Each participant was asked questions regarding knowledge of the effects of the primary hindrance indicators such as gender inequality, discrimination, and underrepresentation. It was noted that participants were not afraid of being candid about experiences; participants freely shared attitudes, beliefs, and opinions about experiences as women in leadership. The following sections summarize participants' responses regarding vital hindrance indicators such as gender inequality, discrimination, and underrepresentation.

Data Collection

Data collection occurred between July 2021 and August 2021. Data were collected through a variety of methods. Questionnaire data were collected using the JotForm system, and in-depth participant interviews were conducted via the Zoom platform. Semi-structured, open-ended questions were asked of each participant, and interviews were recorded with the participant's permission. The interviewer took clarifying observational field notes during the recorded interview and additional notes for the non-recorded portion before recording commenced and after the conclusion. The interviewer asked follow-up questions to ensure an accurate understanding of participants' responses.

The data collection and analysis were done using a qualitative approach, leading to the themes that emerged. The data collection process for the research study involved the following:

- The research setting was conducive to semi-structured and open-ended interview questions and narrative inquiry.
- Participants were able to discuss lived experiences freely and without interruption.
- The use of an audio recording device supported the transcription of the participants' sessions and aided in clarifying stated material.

The interview transcriptions resulted in an in-depth understanding of the research questions' responses. Data from the interviews were analyzed using NVivo 12 software to obtain emergent themes and patterns. The enhanced software coding of the research data consisted of listing and grouping data, reducing and eliminating data, and developing thematic groupings, clusters, and secondary themes. Creswell (2009) indicated that when a researcher relies on manual analysis to sort, organize, and locate words in a qualitative study, it can become tedious and laborious. Creswell stated that data analysis using a qualitative approach may involve a six-step process (Table 5).

Table 5

Analysis Procedure of Data Collected

Steps	Description
1.	Organizing and preparing data for analysis
2.	Exploring Data
3.	Describing the data and searching patterns
4.	Coding materials by topic
5.	Representing data and producing reports
6.	Interpreting the data and building themes grounded in data

Data Transcription

The audio files were reviewed after each interview, and transcription followed immediately. After each transcription was completed, the audio file was listened to again and compared with the transcribed text. The process of listening to the audio recording for the second time and comparing its content with the transcribed text was conducted to confirm the accuracy and authenticity of the transcripts. Transcriptions were sent to participants for review to ensure that their thoughts and words were accurately reflected. While responding was not mandatory, all participants agreed that the transcription accurately reflected expressed perceptions.

According to Eddles-Hirsch (2015), the process of horizontalization assures that every statement has equal value. Thus, horizontalization was used to ensure that each participant's responses and comments were relevant to the topics of gender inequality, discrimination against women, underrepresentation of women, and hindrance to the advancement of women socially, economically, and politically. Each semi-structured interview transcript relevant to the research study was then developed based on the responses. The horizontalization process improved the reduction and elimination of redundant, interchangeable, double-meaning statements. Expressions that occurred during questioning and interviewing were captured and reviewed. Any statements with double meanings and all redundant or interchangeable views were discarded. Each of the expressions was reevaluated to ensure that it could be abstracted and labeled.

The interviews were transcribed based on the order of receipt. The transcripts and data collected were associated with the contact information of the participants. As soon as the data from the interview were collected, data were analyzed for further understanding. The transcribed data were then analyzed together to assure a cumulative idea of the contents. Notes were taken, which were used to annotate common themes and patterns that served as the basis for the coding system used in the NVivo 12 software. Data were gathered through analyzing and examining the transcription, both individually and collectively.

During the study, transcripts were analyzed from the 13 interviews. The study utilized the qualitative research software NVivo 12 to import the transcribed interviews to confirm the data analysis that was initially established through the conceptual framework described in Chapter 1. The qualitative method and NVivo 12 software identified themes associated with educational level, job performance, political views, salaries, and family values. The primary focus was to ensure that the data collected and transcribed addressed the original research questions. Using the NVivo 12 software, the data were classified and then categorized into descriptive units. Data collected from the interviews were analyzed, resulting in gathering myriad perspectives of the participants as they described lived experiences, attitudes, beliefs, and opinions concerning the effect on women who experience gender inequality, discrimination, underrepresentation, and interference to social, economic, and political advancement.

The next step in the data analysis process was interpreting the data collected during the qualitative interview to draw meaning. This was achieved by organizing the findings of the data, explaining the data, and providing an in-depth analysis of how the collected data addressed the research questions in the study. The second step in data analysis was to clarify and put the transcriptions within the context of the study. The textual data consisted of open responses to open-ended questions, which cumulatively constructed a description that explained the overall attitudes, beliefs, and opinions of the participants in the study. Based on the themes that developed, a profound understanding of the effects of the underrepresentation of women in leadership roles emerged.

Research Questions

In response to Research Question 1, How do women's mentorship programs influence women in attaining top leadership positions in private and political sectors?, participants shared that while having a mentoring program may prove beneficial in providing career guidance and psychological support at times, having a sponsor was even more helpful.

Table 6

Research Question 1 Quotations

Research Question	Quotation Reference
RQ1: How do women mentorship programs influence women in attaining top leadership positions in private and political sectors?	"I think that we need more mentorship programs among women." "I have not benefited from female mentorship programs per se. What I find is that I am a natural leader."

Sponsors, whether male or female, can provide significant resources to securing and maintaining leadership positions. Thirty percent of participants did not believe that participating in a mentoring program aided participants in attaining top leadership positions. Participant 2 noted, "I think that we need more mentorship programs among women," while Participant 1 claimed, "I have not benefited from female mentorship programs per se. What I find is that I am a natural leader." This indicates the diversity of opinion among the participants on the issue of women's mentorship programs.

In exploring answers to Research Question 2, the study asked what support women needed to attain successful careers as leaders. Data obtained from responses allowed the study to further explore the themes and patterns by identifying specific aspects of hindrances to the advancement of women socially, politically, and economically.

Table 7

Research Question 2 Quotations

Research Question	Quotation Reference
RQ2: What support women need to attain successful careers as leaders?	"I think we're hurting ourselves because we don't reach out and ask [leaders] for help or even ask each other for guidance."
	"My support system is a group of women [who] has higher education, and they're older than me, so it's easy for me to listen to what they've been through."
	"If there were more women who were in those positions who had those experiences, it would be different because we know how to adapt and change."

Of the 13 participants, 90% (12) expressed that access to leadership opportunities was critical to success. Participant 4 argued, "I think we're hurting ourselves because we don't reach out and ask [leaders] for help or even ask each other for guidance." The vast majority of participants expressed the belief that normalizing women in leadership positions were the most extraordinary support to equality.

At 85% (10), another commonality among the participants was the belief that support systems, including family members and colleagues, play an integral role in women's leadership by supporting dreams and purpose. Participant 2 said, "My support system is a group of women [who] has higher education, and they're older than me, so it's easy for me to listen to what they've been through." Participant 3 stated, "My husband, my mother, even my children have been just a great support system." Participants also discussed the underlying fact that the stereotype that men perform better still exists and makes the discrepancy in pay blatantly evident. It was also noted that although over the last several decades, millions of women have joined the workforce and made considerable gains in educational attainment, too often it is assumed that this pay gap is not evidence of discrimination but is instead a statistical artifact of failing to adjust for factors that may drive earning differences between men and women.

Participants believed these factors—particularly occupational differences between women and men—are often affected by gender bias. A common perception is that the persistent gap reflects a lack of top female leaders and that those now in place often hold lower-paid posts like heads of marketing or human resources. For organizations and companies to change, organizations and companies must add more women at all levels to maintain a diverse pool for promotions (Correll, 2004). Participant 2 stated that "if there were more women in those positions who had those experiences, it would be different because we know how to adapt and change."

In considering Research Question 3 asked how the representation of women in higher levels of leadership impacted the views and beliefs of women's leadership roles. The consensus of the participants was that having diversity in leadership is critical. Participants stated that evolving job needs are empowering women and leveling the playing field. Many believed that the new service economy does not rely on physical strength but skills that often come quickly to women, such as determination, attention to detail, and measured thinking.

Table 8

Research Question 3 Quotations

Research Question	Quotation Reference
RQ3: How does the representation of women in higher levels of leadership impact the views and beliefs of women's leadership roles?	"We isolate ourselves, and I think we're hurting ourselves because we don't reach out and ask for help or even ask each other for guidance." "I happened to be in a skill area that the company valued. And each time they were letting people go, I was in a position where they said, "No, this is a protected position. As a woman, I felt that our time as women in leadership positions was finally coming."

Others shared the belief that the female brain is naturally wired for long-term strategic vision and community building. Participants expressed that having more women in leadership positions may drastically change the landscape of leadership overall.

Participants also discussed that having more women in leadership may increase the understanding of the workforce dynamics, with 75% (10) of participants expressing the belief that it is regrettable that the glass-ceiling theory still exists. The 25% (3) balance perceived some growth in women being accepted in leadership roles. One participant noted that becoming the first female coroner had impacted how women leaders are viewed in a "man's role." Participant 4 stated, "We isolate ourselves, and I think we're hurting ourselves because we don't reach out and ask for help or even ask each other for guidance." In addition, another participant expressed that she was in "a cultural change as well as a business change." The participant added:

> I happened to be in a skill area that the company valued. And each time they were letting people go, I was in a position where they said, 'No, this is a protected position.' As a woman, I felt that our time as women in leadership positions was finally coming.

This is to signify that having a better representation of women in higher levels of leadership may create role models who can offer guidance and pave the way for other women.

More defined questions accompanied the research questions to ensure the participants understood the questions entirely, such as: Do you know the meaning of "perceptions?" and What does belief mean to you? The purpose of these defining questions was to determine participants' understanding of the terms perceptions and beliefs and contextual meaning related to women's limitations in advancement roles politically, economically, and socially. Data collected from the responses to question 3 provided avenues for further exploration of specific aspects of the underrepresentation of women. Each participant was asked to explain her understanding of the terms perceptions and beliefs and to support her response by providing an interpretation. If the participant did not understand the operational definition of underrepresentation, she was assured that an operational explanation of perceptions and beliefs would be provided to offer a contextual viewpoint for the interview.

Using Research Question 4 asked participants what factors motivate or limit women in attaining top leadership positions in the private and public sectors. The concerns were complicated, nuanced, and challenging to separate, according to all participants. There was a notion that both structural problems (policies and work practices) that create hurdles for women and cultural issues (beliefs, prejudices, and values) that generate biased judgments about women's capacity to lead successfully need to be better understood. Participants stated that when women are comfortable and believe in an organization, they may be the most prominent promoters of organizations as a good place for women to work.

Table 9

Research Question 4 Quotations

Research Question	Quotation Reference
RQ4: What are the various factors motivating or limiting women in attaining top leadership positions in the private and public sectors?	"When women are comfortable and believe in an organization, women may be the most prominent promoters of organizations as a good place for women to work."
	"Women may be more likely to think that organizations have sought broad input on the root causes of gender inequality and has put real effort into this issue."

Moreover, another participant stated that "Women may be more likely to think that organizations haves sought broad input on the root causes of gender inequality and has put real effort into this issue."

Using Research Question 5 asked participants how women's family dynamics affected leadership roles as compared to male counterparts. Participants responded that the work environment and home life need to be balanced. Data obtained from question 5 responses allowed the study to explore themes and patterns by identifying specific aspects of the hindrance to women's social advancement. One participant stated:

> Family and career go hand in hand. I had a 4:30 job. I would get out of that and go to school. It was a class [from 6:00-9:00]. [I] had a family. All three is where most people would quit school or work and say, 'I just want to focus on school.'

Multitasking taught me how to be a good leader on the job.

While another participant asserted:

> We should share more with young ladies that you can be married and have children and a career and show them this is how you do it successfully. You don't have to wait until you think that you've achieved a certain level.

This illustrates the belief that balancing family, studies, and career can make one grow to become a strong leader if women have the right mentality.

Due to the gendered prescription of the qualities and actions expected of male leaders, leadership can be a contradictory role for women. As a result, structural impediments confront women in organizations, forming the labyrinth of twists and turns that women leaders must navigate. Moreover, despite labor market participation, many women continue to perform most household duties and childcare. The family's gendered distribution and responsibilities have created a need for some women leaders to work a second shift at home. One participant stated, "When I'm working and talking to my children, I tell them what happens in the profession, that you got to also add to what you do in your personal life." Another participant added, "It's not a stereotype where the female cannot be successful in a career because she has to take care of the home." This indicates that juggling between personal life and a career can be stressful, as handling household chores can be a limitation to performance at the workplace.

Furthermore, participants expressed tension when the female was away from home more than the male. Women believed that the nurturing part of having a woman in the house was missing. One participant stated:

> You must sit down and have an honest discussion or thought with yourself and say, 'What is it that I want? Okay, can you have it all, maybe, but maybe not at

the same level that you want. If you want to get married, start a family, or have raised children, married or not, how will I make all that work?'

The participants shared that these decisions were not ones they believed men would have to ponder.

Table 10

Research Question 5 Quotations

Research Question	Quotation Reference
RQ5: How does a women's family dynamics affect the leadership role compared to her male counterparts?	"When I'm working and talking to my children, I tell them what happens in the profession, that you got to also add to what you do in your personal life." "It's not a stereotype where the female cannot be successful in a career because she has to take care of the home."

Participants felt more disadvantaged because the role and weighty responsibilities required women to be in the home more than their male counterparts.

Results

The data collected from the one-on-one, semi-structured interviews were analyzed to expose the emergent themes and collate patterns from participants' cumulative beliefs, attitudes, and opinions concerning the impact on women who are discriminated against, underrepresented, and prevented from occupying leadership roles. The NVivo 12 software was used in the data analysis process and assisted in coding patterns and uncovering themes from the data collected in the entire interview process. The software allowed the data to be coded, categorized, analyzed, and interpreted to identify dominant themes from the interviews. The participants shared ideas and perspectives concerning key attributes that contributed to the effects women experience when women are discriminated against, underrepresented, and prevented from occupying leadership roles.

Summary of Core Themes

The study participants gave significance and emphasis to the importance of women in leadership roles. The participants believed society informed the standards guiding beliefs, values, attitudes, and other foundational factors. The participants also believed value attributed to women based on society is highly insignificant. The participants indicated that if society did not impose strict standards that consider women second-class citizens, they would not be discriminated against, underrepresented, marginalized, and prevented from assuming leadership roles. The participants believed that society has permeated mindsets that women's leadership ability is not developed to the point where women should rightfully or automatically be seated at higher leadership levels. Participants believed that women who demonstrate attributes societally assigned to men are less accepted and thus not supported. Yet, when women operated in the duality of soft and strong, they were deemed more friendly and worth assuming leadership roles or progressing economically, socially, and politically. After analyzing the collected data, five dominant themes were noted that included *gender preference, politics, religion, education,* and *ethnicity* as the barriers and biases faced by women while attaining leadership positions in governmental organizations and private industries. These five dominant themes are discussed in depth below.

Gender Preference

The study participants indicated that community norms played a significant part in influencing gender preferences regarding women in leadership roles. The participants proffered that the belief that males provide certain qualities that females do not possess is a common ideology in organizations. Several participants stated their belief that males provide satisfactory or tangible returns, primarily in the economic, social, psychological, or religious domains. According to participants, males are preferred to be the successors in the family lineage; the males inherit the family name, wealth, and right to leadership due to cultural practices (Mueller et al., 2017). One participant noted that "there is a cultural bias or belief that, for example, Asians are good at technology. I think we all buy into that and perhaps don't understand that this is coaching and pushing it as truth." Another participant asserted:

> Gender bias is so ingrained in our culture and our community. We have to be willing to assist in the beginning, acknowledge our biases and prejudices, have real conversations with ourselves, and understand what we bring if we are going to talk about the problem by being a part of the solution.

This demonstrates that for women and communities to advance, men need to acknowledge the prejudice in women's leadership and create a culture that appreciates and supports women in developing and leading in different capacities.

Table 11

Dominant Themes: Gender Preference

Theme	Illustrative Quotes
Gender Preference	"Gender bias is so ingrained in our culture and our community. We have to be willing to assist in the beginning, acknowledge our biases, our prejudices, be able to have real conversations with ourselves, and understand what we bring if we are going to talk about the problem by being a part of the solution."
	"There is a cultural bias or belief that, for example, Asians are good at technology. I think we all buy into that and perhaps don't understand that this is coaching and pushing it as truth."

Politics

The participants were cognizant of the role gender and politics play in women's leadership because each indicated that the relationship is complicated. The participants affirmed that women strongly believe that men have better opportunities for leadership positions in business and politics, even as majorities state that men and women make equally good leaders. However, there is little consensus on why women remain underrepresented in these fields (Forbes Coaches Council, 2018). One participant claimed:

> Men have promoted and brought along those who were like them. And so I think that as more women and more minority women move, hopefully, we will bring more who are like us along, since they are just but a few.

Participants agreed that women's representation in leadership positions in almost all operations sectors is always fewer than men.

Numerous participants acknowledged that politics was one of the tools used by males to keep women from attaining natural leadership potential. The participants explained that women do not often advance socially, economically, and politically because men have used politics to prevent involvement in community issues. One participant emphasized that:

> We sit down and have a glass of wine to talk about the struggles that sometimes come with being a woman in politics. [There is] someone that I've been able to confide in from a political standpoint. Changing that idea and navigating that space as a female for the first time has been challenging.

Thus, according to participants, men deploy politics to achieve various levels of dominance and control over women's ability to reach certain levels of leadership in the political spectrum. Yet, some women also become barriers to other women who want to ascend into political space and make influential policies for the communities. One participant recalled:

> At first, I played the dumb game. Then I found out it was my girl trying to undermine me; it wasn't the guys. You are trying to pull left to get this done, but you get a call that we have to meet with the same people trying to undo what you have done. Speaking politically now, it is challenging.

This example indicates that when women position women in leadership platforms, they may experience resistance from fellow women. Participants added that this may allow men to capitalize on such situations to position men to get contested positions.

Table 12

Dominant Themes: Politics

Theme	Illustrative Quotes
Politics	"Men have promoted and brought along those who were like them. And so, I think that as more women and more minority women move, hopefully, we will bring more who are like us along since they are just but a few."
	"[There is] someone that I've been able to confide in from a political standpoint. We sit down, have a glass of wine to just talk about the struggles that sometimes come with being a woman in politics. Working to change that idea and navigate that space as a female for the first time has been hard."
	"At first, I played the dumb game. Then I found out it was my girl trying to undermine me; it wasn't the guys. You are trying to pull left to get this done, but you get a call that we must meet with the same people trying to undo what you have done. Speaking politically now, it is challenging."

Religion

The study participants indicated that traditional and modern religious practices fail to help women who struggle to liberate other women from gender inequality, discrimination against women, underrepresentation of women in leadership roles, and advancing economically, socially, and politically (Koehler & Calais-Haase, 2018).

According to participants, religion does not assign essential functions to women, such as ritual, leadership, and social positions. One participant asserted:

Every time I go to church, it just bugs me. So often, when you go to church, women are singing, and they're not necessarily trained. They have beautiful voices, and they're singing. But when I look at the skill base, the trained musicians on the lead are heavily male. Whether white or black, the bass guitars, the guitars, the percussionist, the director, they're heavily male.

Another acknowledged:

When I got to college to do my course, I had a lot of emails with my church. Many people would tell me that I could do whatever I wanted in the job market as I had potential. But in church, I was never allowed to lead anywhere for personal growth. That did limit me as I was not exposed early into leadership.

The feedback obtained from participants indicates that religious circles only appreciate women following the lead but not being in the lead and that rarely are women given influential leadership positions in those spaces to demonstrate that women are equally capable. Hence, with a small percentage of women leading large churches, participants stated it was due primarily to institutionalized patriarchal leadership models in many worship houses. However, participants asserted that more women of faith are redefining leadership in places of worship, providing essential role models for young congregants, and pushing to transform gender inequality from within religious traditions. One participant recalled:

Most of us grew up knowing that there was a church. Some of us grew up with our parents and grandparents, who were taking us to church. Now they are allowing me to talk to people about my journey to leadership as they believe I'm successful in my career.

This statement indicates that the participant perceives that having a progressive career makes one an essential role model in the community who can inspire other members to pursue individual dreams.

Table 13

Dominant Themes: Religion

Theme	Illustrative Quotes
Religion	"Every time I go to church, it just bugs me. Often, when you go to church, women are singing and they're not necessarily trained. They have beautiful voices, and they're singing. But when I look at the skill base, the trained musicians on the lead are heavily male. Whether white or black, the bass guitars, the guitars, the percussionist, the director, they're heavily male."
	"When I got to college to do my course, I had a lot of emails with my church. Many people would tell me that I could do whatever I wanted in the job market as I had potential. But in church, I was never allowed to lead anywhere for personal growth. That did limit me as I was not exposed early into leadership."
	"Most of us grew up knowing that there was a church. Some of us grew up with our parents and grandparents, who were taking us to church. Now they are allowing me to talk to people about my journey to leadership as they believe I'm successful in my career."

Education

Those study participants who were 35–50 years of age felt compelled to seek further education beyond college. Participants recognized that women have been earning more college and post-secondary degrees than men, contributing to considerable job growth for women. Participants acknowledged that the world is continuing to change, and if one aspires to thrive in the job market, one must change with it. All participants acknowledged the importance of having education credentials since a lack of credentials limits one from attaining leadership positions. One participant lamented:

> I have all this experience, but I did not have the education to go along with it, so [I] systematically took classes that would put me in that position to get where I need to be to be able to obtain some of these higher-level positions.

This response indicated the necessity of attaining higher education or credentials to progress along the career ladder.

Computer skills have been noted as one of the leading and necessary skills in the current digital working environment. Lack of these skills can be a significant barrier to achieving leadership positions in organizations in a market with rapid technology growth. Moreover, it was recognized that artificial intelligence might likely impact almost every occupation; therefore, being as marketable and educated with new skills as possible may help participants prosper in the ever-changing employment arena. One participant remembered:

> I remember in my previous organization when they upgraded the system and needed to promote someone to lead the team, but since I do not have advanced computing skills, I missed the chance even if I was ripe for promotion. Not once have I seen older employees being promoted over younger employees when leadership positions required advanced computer skills.

This indicates that lack of advanced computer skills can be a considerable hindrance to attaining leadership positions in organizations since the future of the workplace will be highly computerized.

Although statistically, women have more degrees than men, the pay inequity between the genders remains entrenched within organizations. One participant alleged:

> We live in a world that believes that the woman is insubordinate. And that women shouldn't be in the leadership. You hear about it when it comes to paying in certain professions than others. But I think more and more men realize that women have something to offer the world.

This is an indication of the belief that bias exists when determining compensation packages. When gender is a factor, male and female employees with similar credentials are entitled to different packages, with fewer women (Mueller et al., 2017).

Table 14

Dominant Themes: Education

Dominant Theme	Illustrative Quotes
Education	"I have all this experience, but I did not have the education to go along with it, so I systematically took classes that would put me in that position to get where I need to be to be able to obtain some of these higher-level positions."
	"I remember in my previous organization when they upgraded the system and needed to promote someone to lead the team, but since I do not have advanced computing skills, I missed the chance even if I was ripe for promotion. Not once have I seen older employees being promoted over younger employees when there were leadership positions that required advanced computer skills."
	"We live in a world that believes that the woman is insubordinate. And that women shouldn't be in the leadership. You hear about it when it comes to paying in certain professions than others. But I think more and more men realize that women have something to offer the world."

Ethnicity

Ethnicity is one of the biases and barriers women face while attaining leadership positions in governmental organizations and private industries. This is perceiving a particular group of people affiliated to a specific background as inferior or superior based on the existing stereotypes of cultural misappropriations (DeLisi et al., 2017). Some participants mentioned experiencing resistance to ascend in leadership positions due to the color of their skin color or because of their background. In discussing the hiring of a male colleague, one participant stated:

> Since he came, we were maybe 5% faculty of color in the last five years, which is terrible. Now we're down to 1%. And every Black person in any role of director and above has been gone since he came in. Yeah, we've lost.

Another shared:

> I know I'm not for everybody, and I'm not going to get along with everyone because some people are bringing their biases and their prejudices and their experiences into the workplace in a very negative way. Now, I've been fired; I've been let go because I was too sure of myself as a Black woman, is what she said.

This is an indicator that prejudice created based on an individual's skin tone limits some people from progressing to leadership positions.

Table 15

Dominant Themes: Ethnicity

| Dominant Theme | Illustrative Quotes |

| Ethnicity | "Since he came in the last five years, we were maybe five percent faculty of color, which is terrible. Now we're down to one percent. And every black person in any role of director and above has been gone since he came in. Yeah, we've lost." |
| | "I know I'm not for everybody, and I'm not going to get along with everyone because some people are bringing their biases and their prejudices and their experiences into the workplace in a very negative way. Now, I've been fired; I've been let go because I was too sure of myself as a black woman, is what she said." |

Chapter Summary

This study investigated the underrepresentation of women through the lived experiences and perceptions of 13 study participants from across the United States. The purpose of the study was to explore how biases and stereotypical views of female behavior affect women who aspire to high-ranking leadership roles in governmental organizations and private industries. The study focused on gaining descriptions of each participant's leadership experiences and how she perceived bias, stereotyping, and prejudice as she progressed through a career in leadership in her chosen field. Data were collected through in-depth interviews. Semi-structured and open-ended questions were asked of each participant. Based on the data collected through a semi-structured, audio-recorded interview, the experiences and perceptions of the participants were transcribed verbatim using NVivo 12 software. Transcriptions were analyzed to boost the synthesis and analysis of the interviews. The investigated findings of the perspectives and experiences of study participants may create an awareness that can guide leaders in the workplace to begin evaluating benchmarks and performance indicators that may assist women in advancing socially, economically, and politically and occupying leadership roles. The qualitative study results may also assist leaders in instituting new methods, approaches, and policies that will help women in achieving gender equality, eliminating discrimination against women, and granting women full representation. The data analysis resulted in five dominant themes, gender preference, politics, religion, education, and ethnicity, as the women's barriers and biases while attaining leadership positions in governmental organizations and private industries.

In Chapter 4, the study provided a review of the data analysis process and research findings. In addition, a connection to the central research questions of the study was provided. The results obtained from the study have appropriate relevance to better understanding the extent of the effect of inequality, discrimination against women, and the underrepresentation of women. The study's purpose was to examine and explore the factors that hinder women from advancing economically, socially, and politically and from occupying leadership roles. Based on information obtained from the study, it may be possible for leaders to utilize the results in making essential policy changes geared toward those factors that hinder women from achieving economic, social, and political success and from occupying leadership roles. Recommendations from the study's findings may also provide relevant interventions on the factors that hinder women from achieving leadership roles. In Chapter 5, the study provides the conclusion of the research and suggestions for further study.

CHAPTER 5: CONCLUSIONS & SUGGESTIONS FOR FURTHER STUDY

The problem this study sought to address in this qualitative study was the barriers and biases of the female leadership gap, specifically in governmental organizations and private industries. This qualitative study explored biases and barriers faced by women while attaining leadership positions in governmental organizations and private industries. This study closely examined the lived experiences of women who successfully navigated a road to executive leadership to better understand successful strategies, while acknowledging the obstacles or limitations experienced.

Through the study, participants reflected on instances that helped cultivate a leadership journey, exploring how personal involvements provided context for creating a philosophy of what leaders of any gender may do. Participants conveyed significant meaning regarding the extent of the support received from others, reflecting on its impact on personal and professional growth. Many women admitted that a critical component of leadership path was a desire to make a difference in the community or contribute to the greater good regardless of the barriers and biases faced.

The study's findings revealed evidence of barriers and biases against female leadership in executive and director positions, as well as favoritism for male leadership at the executive levels. This disparity may also be due to the large number of competent male and female candidates competing for executive leadership roles. Although there have historically been numerous advances in women's positions and accomplishments, there has been little change in the number of female executives (Gillard & Okonjo-Iweala, 2020). While overt prejudice in organizations may be less prevalent than it was 30 years ago, studies on women's subjective experiences (Catalyst, 2004; Kray et al.,

2017; Selzer & Robles, 2019; Silver, 2018) indicated that bias has not been eradicated (Southeastern Oklahoma State University, 2020).

According to Hoyt and Simon (2017), women in leadership positions face the risk of being mistreated or criticized because of a negative stereotype connected with being a woman. These threats "can undermine women's sense of belonging in a field, self-confidence, job attitudes, and motivation and desire to pursue success within the field" (Hoyt & Simon, 2017, p. 17). The authors found relationships "can both increase a sense of social belonging and inoculate people's sense of self against identity threats" (p. 18). Professional relationships should work like any other inter-personal relationship: thriving on transparency, honesty, and mutual respect. A basis for a more inclusive and diverse workforce may be established by working together to build these types of professional connections.

Many women leaders address barriers and prejudices both emotionally and logically (Gillard & Okonjo-Iweala, 2020). As a result, female executives may unintentionally reinforce male leadership stereotypes. Women, who nationally have more undergraduate, postgraduate, and professional degrees than men remain underrepresented in positions of power and leadership in both the public and commercial sectors (Skewes et al., 2018). Women, while qualified, are not always offered the same opportunities in the workplace due to prejudice, discrimination, and incorrect assumptions about their credentials for executive leadership (Gillard & Okonjo-Iweala, 2020). Women are underrepresented 10:1 in executive and board roles (Kochar & Venkateswaran, 2020). Although overt and conscious forms of discrimination and prejudice are becoming less common, more subtle types of bias and discrimination continue to be a barrier to the advancement of female leaders to executive positions of leadership (U.S. Agency for International Development, 2019).

Specific barriers and challenges exist that hinder women from securing leadership positions in organizations. Five dominant themes were noted that included: (1) gender preference, (2) politics, (3) religion, (4) education, and (5) ethnicity as the most prevalent biases and barriers faced by women seeking leadership positions in governmental organizations and private industries.

There are myriad qualified female leaders available (Martineau & Mount, 2019). In the United States, women make up more than half of the workforce. In terms of bachelor's and master's degrees, women outnumber men, and in the earning of medical and legal degrees are equal (Warner et al., 2018). However, men are far more likely than women to achieve the highest-paid and most prominent leadership roles, from corporate boardrooms to Congress, healthcare corporations to the courts, non-profit organizations to institutions (Gillard & Okonjo-Iweala, 2020).

The purpose of this qualitative phenomenological research study was to explore the lived experiences of women overlooked for leadership positions in the workplace. In this chapter, the study outlines the research's summary, discussion, and conclusions, the theoretical implications of the results, and the practical and future implications. A discussion of the strength and weaknesses of the study, recommendations for future research, and a summary conclude this chapter.

Summary of Study

Research has shown that women experience leadership differently than men (Eagly & Karau, 2002; Storberg-Walker & Haber-Curran, 2017). When circumstances are challenging in an organization, hiring a skilled leader to guide people through a crisis is regarded as desirable (Watson & Detjen, 2021). Selection panels seeking compassionate talent, which is perceived as feminine, were more likely to choose a woman to lead during trying times (Gillard & Okonjo-Iweala, 2020). Social role theory and role congruity theory have been used to explain how bias and prejudice create a different work environment for women because of the dissonance a female presence makes when she assumes leadership roles (Eagly & Karau, 2002; Moore & Wang, 2017; Seo et al., 2017; White, 2019; Thorne, 2020). While it is frequently used to explain why women are held back and are unable to advance (Eagly & Karau, 2002), in this research, role congruity theory was useful in better understanding the gender-based biases experienced by women who had successfully achieved a top leadership position.

Overview

Although many women have similar qualifications to their male counterparts, research has demonstrated that leadership has historically been a male privilege in the business, political, military, and other social sectors (Eagly & Karau, 2002). Studies have further indicated that women have been underrepresented in managerial positions (Schulz & Enslin, 2014; Tariq & Syed, 2014, 2017; Warner et al., 2018) and those women are less likely than men to advance to the top of a respective fields (Colella & King, 2018; Moreno et al., 2020). Additionally, despite more women acquiring degrees than men (Warner et al., 2018) and performing better than men in the workplace overall (Watson & Detjen, 2021), this does not always influence organizations to entrust women with leadership roles.

Women have unique abilities to balance risk and cope with failure (Watson & Detjen, 2021). With these special abilities and higher education and professional credentials, women are ideal candidates for leadership (Saleem et al., 2017). The imbalance of gender representation in leadership positions inspired the study to investigate the causes of women's underrepresentation in leadership using a sample of 13 women from across the United States.

The study utilized a phenomenological research design to explore the lived experiences of 13 women who were overlooked for leadership positions in the workplace. The central phenomena investigated in this study were the facets that lead to the underrepresentation of women in leadership positions who are as equally qualified as male counterparts. The study utilized qualitative methodology. The methodology was deemed appropriate as it gave voice to participants, allowing women to share experiences. Through this method, the study obtained data through open-ended and conversational communication. Researchers applying this method consider not only what participants think but also why participants think in certain ways.

Data was collected through questionnaires, interviews, and field notes. Questionnaire data were collected using the JotForm system. In-depth interviews with participants were completed utilizing the Zoom platform. Open-ended questions were employed to collect opinions and insights from 13 women across the United States to explore the perceived and experienced causes of women's underrepresentation in leadership. The interview questions were specifically designed to reveal the experiences and perceptions of women who have faced challenges of competing with men in the workplace. A purposive sampling method was utilized to select participants.

To invite women who met the designed criteria to participate in the study, social media platforms were utilized. Once interest was expressed by a potential participant, informed consent forms were distributed via email. The study ensured that potential participants were well briefed about the study's purpose to ensure that they had all information needed to make an informed decision to consent to participate. Upon receipt of the executed informed consent form, a second contact was made through email to distribute the questionnaire. When the completed questionnaire was received, participants were contacted to coordinate a date and time for the individual interview. Participants were given an informed consent form, upon which, upon signing and returning, indicated that the participant was willing to participate in the study.

The sample was composed of women between the ages of 30 and 65 from various ethnic, socioeconomic, and religious backgrounds. The participants were selected through purposive sampling of women who identified as leaders based on current or previous job experiences and positions. Interviews were recorded with participants' permission, and were transcribed and analyzed using NVivo 12 software. The following research questions guided the study:

- RQ1: How do women mentorship programs influence women in attaining top leadership positions in private and political sectors?
- RQ2: What support do women need to attain successful careers as leaders?
- RQ3: How does the representation of women in higher levels of leadership impact society's views and beliefs on women's leadership roles?
- RQ4: What are the various factors motivating or limiting women in attaining top leadership positions in private and public sectors?

- RQ5: How does a woman's family dynamics affect her leadership role compared to her male counterparts?

The study explored and offered a potential explanation for the underrepresentation of women in leadership roles and discussed the role of gender stereotyping regarding the smaller number of women in leadership positions than men. The research is relevant to all women who have been overlooked for advancements to management roles at companies. In the United States, women have earned degrees equal to or greater than men, and perform similarly to or better than male counterparts (Zenger & Folkman, 2021)

The findings of this study may provide firms and organizations with a better understanding of qualifications and leadership attributes the women who work in facilities hold. The potential contribution of this study to women's leadership research may also result in more women being promoted to leadership positions previously solely available to men.

Conclusions & Discussion

Rebuffing gendered social norms can have real consequences (Save the Children, 2021). As mentioned previously, when a person dares to venture into regions of nonconformity, the benefits must be carefully weighed against the disadvantages (Okonjo-Iweala, 2020). For the unprepared or unsupported, the subtle cues embedded in gender bias can discourage one from attempting promotion (Nordell & Serkez, 2021). In this section, conclusions and discussions were based on the research findings in theoretical, practical, and future implications.

Women in this study encountered gender biases and showed resilience by adapting to environments and adopting strategies that minimized or avoided conflict. Thomas (2020) referred to this as a contingent leadership style and found it effective for leaders navigating challenging cultural environments. Unfortunately, adopting such a strategy is only a short-term solution. It does not provide an opportunity for an organization to address a culture change that may be needed to create a work environment that embraces women in leadership roles (Eagly & Carli, 2007; Ibarra et al., 2013; Williams & Dempsey, 2017; Zahneis, 2020).

Theoretical Implications

The findings in this study support arguments advanced by the role congruity theory applied in this study. Proponents of the theory suggest that groups are positively evaluated when attributes are recognized to align with the group's social roles (Eagly & Karau, 2002). In this sense, prejudice towards female leaders results from the incongruity between the attributes linked with the female's gender stereotype and the characteristics related to the typical leadership (Eagly & Karau, 2002). The study participants indicated that community norms greatly influenced gender preference. Society believes that men possess some qualities that women do not have, bringing about gender inequality in organizations (Chamorro-Premuzic & Gallop, 2020). Gender inequality relates to unequal opportunities within organizations (Sampson & Gresham, 2017). Mueller et al. (2017) stated that males often step right into leadership due to cultural practices. The results of the present study indicated that men are preferred to be successors in the family lineage and inherit the family wealth.

The conceptual framework can be linked to the role congruity theory. Proponents of the theory assert that a group is positively evaluated because its characteristics align with the social roles of the group (Eagly & Diekman, 2005). A significant barrier preventing women from attaining leadership roles is the perception of women in leadership (Eagly & Karau, 2002). Eagly and Karau (2002) argued women leaders are perceived less positively than male leaders. The social roles of women make women perceived in lower status positions than men (Lyness & Grotto, 2018). Lyness and Grotto (2018) asserted stereotypes contribute to gender inequality in leadership. This study's conceptual framework contributes to role congruity theory by deepening the literature about gender stereotyping. The findings offer deeper insight into the role of culture and society on gender stereotyping.

Role congruity theory indicates that women struggle to meet expectations associated with leadership positions (Eagly & Karau, 2002). To illustrate the implications of the role congruity theory on the gender gap in leadership positions, Creswell and Creswell (2018) reported that even in a situation that was gender-neutral, women still emerged as leaders more than men. The results of this study supported such findings as Creswell and Creswell, Eagly and Karau (2002), and other studies that have investigated gender bias in leadership positions.

Practical and Future Implications

The findings in this study indicated that women still receive lower pay than men despite having more degrees. The participants linked the pay inequality between genders to the societal belief that women should remain insubordinate. The finding was consistent with numerous prior studies on gender pay inequality (Martineau & Mount, 2019).

Several researchers focused on gender discrimination in wages to determine whether the returns for skills and job characteristics were more significant for one gender than the other once other determinants of wages were considered. Heidecke et al. (2020) reported that the American workforce still has a relatively large wage gap between men and women which has largely been attributed to gender discrimination. The consequence of this gap is that many women settle for lower-wage positions. Ammerman and Groysberg (2021) noted that men typically get the highest paying jobs and have much progress in careers while women change companies to progress, and others opt to quit careers and start families. The findings from this study demonstrated the gender pay inequality still exists in great numbers. Practitioners may utilize this knowledge to institute policies to address pay inequality in organizations. Specifically, in this study illuminated a common ideology that men possess certain qualities that women do not, which makes men more capable of leading organizations. This dogma leads to a misnomer that men are better suited for leadership. The findings of this study indicated the extent to which gender bias is ingrained in culture and society. Additionally, the research findings suggested that social norms played a significant role in influencing gender stereotyping regarding leadership positions.

The findings also indicated that community norms played a significant role in influencing gender preferences regarding women in leadership roles. Consequently, men have been given priority over women in leadership roles in many organizations. The study participants believed that society informed organizational standards guiding beliefs, values, attitudes, and other foundational factors. The participants believed that value attributed to women based on society is highly insignificant. The participants stated that the strict standards imposed by society have made women considered second-class citizens, hence the discrimination and marginalization from leadership roles. The findings from this study supported the sentiments by Ben-Noam (2018). According to Ben-Noam (2018), women face gender issues in society and the corporate setting. The study noted that these issues are deeply rooted in culture and public policy. These results may assist leaders in instituting new methods, approaches, and policies to help women achieve gender equality, eliminating discrimination, and granting women full representation.

Although this study concerned women who succeeded in attaining leadership positions, there are myriad cases of women who believed the societal consequences were not worth the expense. This is especially troubling when considered through the lens of representative bureaucracy. When women's voices are muted, whether via purposeful or inadvertent methods of being ignored or forgotten, any effort to advance the goal of a representative bureaucracy is hampered. The suppression of women's voices runs counter to building a public format in which social experiences and perspectives that represent society's diversity are accepted.

This research further identified that men played a significant role in denying women from acquiring leadership in politics. The results suggested that men who have taken leadership roles have brought along other men. Participants stated that men use politics to prevent women from getting involved in community issues. However, although some participants stated that men prevented women from securing leadership positions in organization, other participants stated that women also received resistance from fellow women, giving men an opportunity to take advantage of the situation. It was intriguing that some women did not use positional power to draw attention to or actively address the gender bias ingrained in the corporate culture; however, this is not uncommon (Soklaridis et al., 2017). Soklaridis et al. (2017) found that while women may be frustrated with being overlooked or underestimated, women "have come to the conclusion that this is 'the way it is' in our current society, and that as women, we need to adapt and not dwell on things that are not going to change" (p. 261). Cultural prejudices continually favor males and undervalue women. According to self-evaluation surveys, both men and women respond similarly. However, women tend to rate women two points lower than reality, whilst men rate men two points higher (Martin & Phillips, 2019).

The findings aligned with Miller (2016), who argued that leadership is associated with masculine gender role traits such as assertiveness, confidence, and control. Moreover, Creswell and Creswell (2018) noted that women are perceived to lack these masculine characteristics; hence men have a better chance at leadership positions. From these findings, practitioners may promote women's chances of occupying political leadership roles by inviting other women into the political arena.

The results of the present study revealed insights that may influence future studies. According to the results of this study, males are more likely than women to hold leadership positions in corporations because of society's image of women in leadership, particularly female stereotyping. Prior studies (Creswell & Creswell, 2018; Gosling & Mintzberg, 2017) indicated the prevalence of stereotyping as a significant barrier to women occupying leadership roles. Therefore, future studies may investigate society's perceptions regarding women's leadership and examine factors contributing to female stereotyping may be critical to women's advancement. There was no handbook to assist participants in navigating the leadership journey. None of the women suggested that the leadership career had been seamless or straightforward, yet each had successfully navigated a road to the top.

Strengths and Weaknesses

The study employed a qualitative approach to explore the barriers that women in the private and public sectors face while pursuing leadership positions. One of the strengths of this methodology is that it assists researchers in gathering in-depth information about the issue under study (Creswell & Creswell, 2018). Additionally, utilizing open-ended questions in the study allowed the respondents to elaborate upon given answers, yielding more profound and new data. Consequently, the structure and content of the questions helped gain new and deeper insight into the issue under study.

Member checking is another key strength of this study that enhanced the validity of the results. To preserve the quality and trustworthiness of the data analysis, participants were given a copy of the transcript, checked for errors, and confirmed the accuracy of the information provided. The participants were also afforded an opportunity to offer feedback on the individual descriptions to ensure accurate delivery of what was expressed through the interview.

Applying a phenomenological design helped gather detailed descriptions of lived experiences as first-hand information. The study's design allowed findings to emerge as respondents narrated personal experiences. The study's design was a key strength in this study as it allowed for a better understanding of women's subjective experiences. Therefore, through this design, based on the participant's responses, it was possible to determine the underlying factors that contribute to the underrepresentation of women in leadership positions.

Additionally, the study findings were supported by theory and data. The results indicated gender stereotyping was a significant barrier for women in acquiring leadership positions. For instance, one participant stated,

> Gender bias is so ingrained in culture and communities. We must be willing to assist in the beginning, acknowledge our biases, our prejudices, be able to have real conversations with ourselves, and understand what we bring if we are going to talk about the problem by being a part of the solution.

Another participant stated,

> Men have been promoted and brought along those who were like them. And so, I think that as more women and more minority women move, hopefully, we will bring more who are like us along, since they are just but a few.

The finding is attributed to the role congruity theory of prejudice. From this theory, the bias towards women results from the incongruity between the attributes linked with the female gender and the traits related to the typical leadership. A plethora of past studies support the link between gender stereotyping and the underrepresentation of women in leadership (Creswell & Creswell, 2018; Eagly & Karau, 2002; Freund, 2017).

Furthermore, the study findings directly aligned with the research questions. Specifically, to a greater extent, the data collected answered all the research questions identified in the first chapter of the study. For example, the data collected provided detailed information about the factors that motivate and limit women from attaining top leadership positions in private and public organizations. From the findings, the limiting factors ranged from prejudices, to beliefs, to work policies. The same was evident in the data related to other research questions, whereby the data collected provided detailed and new insights concerning women's underrepresentation in leadership positions.

Table 16 outlines factors participants identified in motivating or limiting their ability to gain leadership positions.

MALE LEADERSHIP GAP

Table 16

Emerging Themes

Factor	Motivate	Limit
Male Counterparts	"My male counterparts have set me up to be somewhat of a role model to those coming behind me."	"It's been a big struggle work[ing with] somebody who didn't openly [say] that you're not who I wanted t[o...]"
Developing Inner Mentality	"I've had to talk myself down when my support system couldn't be there.... and I had to draw from my strength." "You've got to figure what you got to.... because as you get older, you don't need so much validation from other people; you validate yourself."	
Racism		"I feel like my workplace is v[ery] racist.... in the last five years, maybe 5% faculty of color, w[as] terrible. Now we're down to 1[...]"
Role Models	"Having role models that have that, are that, and have been there; to be, you have to see it. So, I think role modeling is absolutely essential." "I think role modeling is pretty important. I am on a campus with 67% of my students are black females who need role models other than the mom who worked four jobs and raised ten kids by herself." "The more you see women leading and having balance, you know you don't have to give up everything."	"Especially women who are m[y] counterparts have been more [...] than anything else. And it's ve[ry...]"

However, the current study had some weaknesses. This qualitative study involved gathering responses from conducted interviews. The limited number of participants only provided data on the participants' responses. However, due to the focus of this study being on women who had achieved a leadership position despite barriers and biases, research that emphasized the inability of women to advance was not as relevant.

Additionally, the sample of 13 women used in the research was a limiting factor in the current study's findings. In a qualitative study, large samples are discouraged, as it can result in extensive data making it more difficult to analyze (Creswell & Creswell, 2018). The current study focused on 13 respondents, making it difficult to generalize the results to all women in organizations.

Moreover, the current research findings are limited by the sampling approach used in determining the study participants. Since the sampling was not random, the results cannot be generalized to populations with different dynamics, social and cultural backgrounds, and perceptions.

Recommendations for Future Research

In the current study, the research utilized a purposive sampling approach. Researchers may replicate this study using random sampling to capture different sample characteristics such as family dynamics, social and cultural backgrounds, and perceptions. Additionally, the current research indicated that men are preferred more than women to occupy leadership positions. This study found female stereotyping as a significant barrier for women in obtaining leadership positions; therefore, recommendations investigating the extent to which stereotyping is rooted in private and public organizations and how it impacts women's careers is warranted. Furthermore, in this study used qualitative methodology whereby there was no quantification of the variables. Future scholars studying gender gaps in leadership may choose to quantify some factors to investigate the relationship of different factors with a preference for men in leadership.

The study results revealed that women face many barriers in advancement to top leadership levels. The barriers and biases include gender stereotyping, in which women are perceived as unequipped and unqualified to possess leadership roles. Men are evaluated favorably in holding leadership roles and maintaining organizational confidence. Additionally, the findings indicated that many leadership positions occupied by men disadvantage qualified women from rising to headship positions. Men in leadership positions tend to prioritize fellow men, thus making it hard for women to advance in leadership positions. According to Dezsö and Ross (2012) women leaders increase value to a corporation's bottom line. Dezsö and Ross' study involved 1,500 management data firms that had at least one woman in a senior management position or had no female leadership in senior management at all. The firms' that had at least one woman in senior leadership demonstrated improved performance over the firms that had no women seated in leadership. These results can be explained through an argument, advanced by Watson and Detjen (2021), that women tend to possess unique abilities, which makes them ideal candidates for leadership. Based on these findings and theory, practitioners should implement policies that enhance the entrance of many women into leadership positions.

There are additional practice suggestions for organizations. The first step is to become aware of the prejudices and hurdles that women encounter due to subtle bias in the organization's infrastructure. Intentional action may be done to counteract the effects of gender-based discrimination and to establish an atmosphere that does not suppress or marginalize women's contributions. When a company recognizes that women commonly face social exclusion in the workplace because of being neglected or forgotten, purposeful steps may be made to promote equitable recognition and involvement. One example is ensuring that men and women are represented equally when hiring.

Organizations may select to be more deliberate in efforts to create and train leaders. Although online leadership training is available, it may be more beneficial to collaborate with the human resources department to strategically identify the leadership skills valued in the organization and develop leadership academies that can serve as a place to encourage dialogue and relationships while reinforcing a standard expectation of leadership skills. Another approach is to find formal leadership development programs for senior executives and identify organizations that have intentionally created leadership development designed specifically for women to determine the extent to which the training supported career advancement.

The study further revealed that women need support from colleagues and family members to attain successful careers as leaders. Moreover, it was revealed that giving women access to all leadership opportunities may play a critical role in success as leaders. Ninety percent of participants in the current study expressed that access to all leadership opportunities is crucial in attaining success. Many of the participant's concerns aligned with Chin et al.'s (2020) study that revealed very few female leaders in the top positions of many organizations. The probability of a woman becoming a top leader in an organization is shallow compared to men. Moreover, the study results indicated that because of the likelihood of not locating a similar position, women in senior positions were 20% less likely than males in comparable positions to leave.

Suggestions for future study include considering the experiences of male mentors to female leaders to better understand the philosophy of helping women develop in careers. Researchers can examine the extent to which males observed gender-based conduct from colleagues and how women dealt with it. Another approach is to conduct comparative research focusing on men's leadership journeys and comparing them to those of women.

Scholars may also select to explore the perceptions of males who worked for women leaders and the extent to which males' experiences informed or modified opinions of women's capacity to lead and whether it influenced how to help other women develop. As Ely et al. (2011) examined leadership development to better understand the complexities of gender dynamics associated with women becoming leaders and advancing into leadership roles. Expanding on this research in conjunction with other areas, such as senior male leadership involvement, would provide an opportunity for additional research to understand better the interaction of several variables and any associated findings regarding the barriers and biases that women face when pursuing leadership positions.

Further research on women in their early careers would be beneficial to gain a better understanding of the factors that influence their career growth, both positively and negatively. The PricewaterhouseCooper (PwC) study, *The Female Millennial: A New Era of Talent* (Flood, 2015), illustrates the career stage differences between millennial women at the start of their careers with 0 to 3 years in the workforce, mid-stage careers with 4 to

8 years in the workforce, and established careers with 9 or more years in the workforce. A continuation of this study, or variations on this study, would be critical to continue elaborating the differences between men and women early in their careers and as they increasingly pursue senior leadership roles.

The findings indicated that normalizing women in leadership positions may enhance women's success in leadership careers. Therefore, practitioners should put policies in place to enable women to compete for top positions against male counterparts. A significant stride that a company can make is to acknowledge and highlight the leadership that women provide. This constitutes a deliberate, yet indirect, technique aimed to counteract gender prejudice and change social expectations of women as leaders. Nominating women for recognition is another specialized technique that helps guarantee that women's work is evaluated alongside males.

Chapter Summary

According to Gillard and Okonjo-Iweala (2020), "From childhood and throughout adulthood, socialization and stereotyping are part of what shapes women and men, including their leadership styles" (p. 31). In this chapter, the study outlined the summary, provided discussion, and conclusions, discussed the theoretical implications of the results, and offered practical and future implications. In addition, she presented the strengths and weaknesses of the study and recommendations for future research. Theoretically, this research added to the literature related to role congruity theory. Specifically, the study revealed that women are perceived less favorably than men as potential occupants of leadership roles and that behaviors that fulfill the prescribed leader role are evaluated less favorably when a woman enacts it. Findings from this study indicated that community norms play a significant role in gender stereotyping by placing men as the head and women as subordinates.

Practically, the study results provided insights that may positively impact women's lives in leadership positions and enhance the participation of women in leadership. The findings on barriers that hinder women from rising to leadership positions may help organizations develop and implement policies that can improve women's representation in leadership. Moreover, supporting women to succeed in leadership roles may help those holding leadership positions as practitioners to implement policies that ensure future female leaders are adequately supported in their roles.

This research yielded four key recommendations. The first was that business organizations must create an atmosphere that encourages women to advance to top positions. The second recommendation was that women be compensated and positioned in corporate jobs based on fair talent management. Third, women should be coached and mentored, but there must also be an emphasis on sponsorship. Fourth, there should be a more significant emphasis on training practical leadership qualities in business groups.

Future studies may build on the existing research design by examining additional geographic locations, assessing other jobs, labels, and industries, and employing various factors. Future research may also explore additional psychological and social hurdles that female executives face ascending the corporate ladder. Finally, future researchers may investigate other successful methods of delivering education and leadership curriculum to business groups.

The current study has numerous strengths and weaknesses related to the methodology used. Strengths included using a qualitative method and open-ended questions, which helped gather in-depth information about the issue under study. The study weaknesses included that the study findings cannot be generalized due to the sample size and the sampling technique used. In this chapter, the study outlined recommendations for future studies, including replicating the current study using a random sampling technique and investigating the extent to which stereotyping is rooted in private and public organizations and how it has impacted women's careers.

www.ingramcontent.com/pod-product-compliance
Lightning Source LLC
LaVergne TN
LVHW011949070526
838202LV00054B/4850